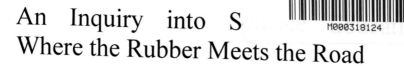

An Inquiry into S
Where the Rubber Meets the Road

An Inquiry into Science Education, Where the Rubber Meets the Road

Richard N. Steinberg
City College of New York, USA

SENSE PUBLISHERS
ROTTERDAM/BOSTON/TAIPEI

A C.I.P. record for this book is available from the Library of Congress.

ISBN: 978-94-6091-688-5 (paperback)
ISBN: 978-94-6091-689-2 (hardback)
ISBN: 978-94-6091-690-8 (e-book)

Published by: Sense Publishers,
P.O. Box 21858,
3001 AW Rotterdam,
The Netherlands
www.sensepublishers.com

Printed on acid-free paper

TABLE OF CONTENTS

PREFACE

You can know the name of a bird in all the languages of the world, but when you're finished, you'll know absolutely nothing whatever about the bird... So let's look at the bird and see what it's doing — that's what counts. I learned very early the difference between knowing the name of something and knowing something.[1]

  - Richard Feynman

HOW LAKEETA CALCULATES THE VELOCITY OF A CAR MOVING WITH VELOCITY 9.5 M/S

It was a great struggle getting my high school physics students to turn in their homework, even when I asked simple, rote questions. It was an even greater struggle when I asked challenging, contextual questions. "It is too hard." "I tried, but couldn't do it." "What homework? I didn't know there was any homework." I gave everyone more and more time, more and more chances, and more and more help and hints. I was available to anyone who wanted extra help any time. The homework was an important part of their grade for the class. Almost all my students wanted to pass and here were some easy points. It was confusing to me why so few submitted their homework. There appeared to be little investment and certainly little success.

Recognizing the need to get the students going and on board, I made the homework easier and easier, more like the "fill in the blank" type that they were used to. In other words I pandered. I lowered academic standards.

Eventually, partly in frustration and partly to make a point, I decided to include the following question (verbatim) as one of the problems:

A car moves with a constant velocity of 9.5 m/s. What is the velocity of the car?

I wanted the class to see that they should read the question, see what was right in front of them, and understand what is being asked. On an intellectual level, I thought that I could convince everyone that they could get started on problems by reading them and thinking about them. On a practical level, I thought that everyone could get some credit on the homework and work towards passing. I was therefore disappointed when few students submitted the obvious answer to the question about the velocity of the car.[2] Like many other first year teachers, I blamed the kids, the school, and the families. Most of all though, I blamed myself.

---

[1] Feynman, R. (1969). What is science. *Phys. Teach.*, 7.
[2] 9.5 m/s.

Lakeeta was an average performing student. All year I had to point out basic rule infractions (such as eating or texting in class) to her. She let me know bluntly that she did not like to be told what to do. Whenever I asked Lakeeta a physics question to try to get her to understand something, she reminded me that I was the teacher and that I should be giving her answers, not asking her questions. I found humor in my relationship with Lakeeta. I think we both enjoyed our banter and we got along okay. Despite her requests, I never stopped doing what I thought was best to try to get her to succeed. In return, she never stopped eating, texting, and grumbling.

Lakeeta was not very inquisitive about the subject matter and did not seem to care about learning physics, but she tried to get all of her homework in and wanted to pass the class. Like many of my students, she was a product of the system. To her, homework (and class work) was a means of accumulating points. If she looked beyond her report card grade at all, it was about being able to do what she thought was important to prepare for the end of year culminating state exam. To her that meant being told what she had to know. It meant being given the explicit procedures needed to answer the questions. I pleaded with Lakeeta explicitly and implicitly to work towards meaningful understanding of science. I tried to teach her that this was critical to real success. This was foreign to Lakeeta.

One way or another, Lakeeta was able to do much of her homework without me every time, but she sought me out for the problem above about the car. This was the one troubling her. She came to extra help. "I could not do this one because I do not know which formula to use."

Lakeeta solved her homework problems with strategies that I saw my college physics students use. Which formula had the matching symbols? Which of the problems in the book had comparable surface features? Lakeeta was not alone in her confusion. Lakeeta's struggle with the car question was not a quirk or an exception. It was a representative outcome of the way many students approached learning in school.

I asked Lakeeta to read the question back to me. She did, albeit with a little attitude. I just looked at her quietly, knowing that she would get annoyed at me. She did not disappoint. After a pause I asked her to read it again, but asked her this time to pay attention to what she was reading. After a short time, she smiled at me. Apparently she understood, both the problem and my point.

DIARY OF A SABBATICAL

As a college professor, it is common to take a sabbatical to travel, write, or research. I spent my sabbatical year as a full time public high school science teacher in a poor neighborhood in New York City. Many colleagues reacted with amazement. Some reacted with horror. Almost all expressed admiration and respect.[3]

For more than 20 years, I have been a physicist and a science educator, primarily at the college level. My research is on understanding and improving the learning of science, from elementary school science through quantum physics. Since 1999 I have been Professor in the School of Education and the Department of Physics and Program Director of Science Education at City College of New York (CCNY). In that time I have had the privilege of working with hundreds of K-12 students, with over a thousand science teachers in and around New York City, and with even more college science students who are graduates of the city school system. I wanted to improve my ability to work with all these groups. Choosing to spend my sabbatical where the rubber meets the road was an easy decision.

In the following 12 chapters, I give a diary of my 12 months away from being a college professor. Anyone who teaches high school science, particularly in an urban setting, will likely recognize the accounts as unsurprising. All of these examples, stories, quotes, and data are genuine and representative, including what I wrote about Lakeeta. However, to present 12 critical themes of science education coherently by chapter, I have shifted some of the chronology around. I have also added experiences from the college level and from other K-12 schools in which I have taught, worked, or volunteered. For obvious reasons, I have changed some details which have no bearing on the substance of the accounts. For example, all names are pseudonyms, usually (although not always) reflective of the gender and race of the person. Minor other changes have been made so that schools, students, and teachers with whom I have worked are not readily identifiable.

PERSPECTIVE

When discussing education, everyone brings a perspective which colors the way events are interpreted. I am no different. The above quote by Richard Feynman, a renowned scientist, educator, author, and Nobel Prize winning physicist, is revealing of my perspective. So are the quotes at the beginning of each chapter by other great scholars, scientists, and cultural figures. Each quote ties to the theme of the chapter.

Instructional strategies described in and after each chapter are also revealing of my perspective. In particular, I have frequently used the curricula of Prof. Lillian McDermott and the Physics Education Group at the University of Washington, which I consider exemplary.[4] With these curricula, students are actively engaged in activities where they build a functional understanding of the subject. Instructional

---

[3] I wish that admiration and respect would be given to the many wonderful teachers who do this every year. I wish that this admiration and respect would then be translated into meaningful support, resources, and ongoing professional development.

[4] I had the privilege of working as part of this group as a postdoctoral research associate from 1992-1995.

strategies are based on what is known about how students learn and address specific difficulties that students have.

Most of all, my perspective is that the very highest academic standards and accountability need be paramount. Any policy that compromises high achievement of students must be reconsidered. I make no secret of my worries about recent and current trends in education which come under the banner of "standards" and emphasize "high stakes testing." My observations as well as my systematic research have created a perspective that these trends are functionally moving students towards rote and authoritarian learning. I see a focus on a limited view of math and literacy and no meaningful emphasis on science and reasoning. I see results completely counter to high academic standards and accountability. I see what is happening in education as problematic. I see doing nothing about it as worse.

Despite my perspective, in this book I have avoided the oft-cited phrase about American education being a "mile wide and an inch deep." I have also avoided the "research has shown," "in the published literature," and "statistics indicate" approach to writing. High quality research is paramount in meaningful educational reform. Unfortunately, too often I have seen these phrases point carelessly to data which are subject to very different interpretations. These phrases are therefore often followed by conflicting perspectives, depending on whatever point the author is trying to make. So instead I have elected to make this book a narrative of my specific experiences and my direct interpretations. *All* of the experiences and interpretations are representative of what I saw on sabbatical and what I see in education today. They are genuine and real. That said, research has shown that my interpretations are consistent with what is prominent in the published literature and statistics indicate that students learn better when using the instructional strategies which are in opposition to the mile wide and inch deep approach.[5]

MATTHEW, RUSSELL, MAKENZIE, AND LILY

Matthew, Russell, Makenzie, and Lily are the only children names in this book that are not pseudonyms. They are the real names of my own children. There is so much that I want for them, some of which relate closely to my work. With respect to my sabbatical, it was particularly exciting to me that my oldest child Matthew was simultaneously taking the same standard New York State high school physics class that I was teaching (in a different school).

At various times, I have heard from one (or more) of my children that when they grow up they want to be a doctor, engineer, executive, judge, lawyer, military officer, pilot, scientist, and teacher.[6] In none of these professions is the training that Lakeeta is used to helpful. These professionals do not work in isolation on de-

---

[5] In other forums I follow a careful research paradigm. I share detailed findings and compelling interpretations built on work of other scholars and researchers. My work, and that of so many others, unambiguously inform and support the main ideas which are presented in this book.

[6] Curiously, I have never heard professor.

contextualized short answer problems with no access to resources of information. Rarely in these professions would there be reward for identifying the technical name of something not understood or for plugging numbers into an obscure formula which might or might not be relevant. Instead, these professionals work as part of a team on meaningful, complex problems while skillfully navigating through vast amounts of diverse information. Rewards come from being able to think critically and communicate skillfully.

The training that Lakeeta is getting is not helpful. In my opinion, it is actually harmful. And my concerns about a poor education are not tied to career choice for Lakeeta. When I think about what preparation leads to a good doctor, engineer, executive, judge, lawyer, military officer, pilot, scientist, and teacher, these are the same skills that benefit workers in all arenas. They are also skills of value for customers and merchants, voters and politicians, friends and neighbors, and just about everyone else.

I do not think about how the *perception* of education can be improved as my children go through their school years, I think about how education can *really* be improved. My year in the high school, coupled with my long and diverse related work, has given me insight into the way things are and the way things could be. When I think of failings in education and how to fix them, my children's welfare is a strong motivating factor.

FORMAT OF BOOK

In Part 1 of this book, I describe the beginning of my sabbatical, before teaching in the high school. I give a summary of a summer program for high achieving New York City high school students. In this program it is evident that even the best and most motivated students are not learning science in their schools. However, after they experience a very different learning environment, it becomes clear that real learning is possible. This summer program explores goals of science education, serves as a motivation for much of my work, and frames the rest of the book. Also in Part 1 I describe other relevant motivating experiences. These include teaching college physics, working with high school science teachers, and my own formal preparation to become certified to teach high school science in New York City. I use all of these motivating experiences to present my perspective on what is meant by inquiry.

In Part 2, the chapters each describe a month of my teaching high school during the school year. Each chapter delves into a theme in education largely through presentation of vignettes, such as the one about Lakeeta. There are examples where student performance is alarming. There are examples where educational experiences are exemplary. In total, the chapters reveal my sabbatical experience teaching in the high school.

In Part 3 I both look back and look forward. I reflect on my sabbatical and what I would do differently if I could do it all over again. I relate what I learned to implications for teacher preparation, science education, and systemic change. I also describe how the community of science educators needs to keep the conversation going and move towards education reform.

At the end of each chapter is a reflection on the chapter theme. There is a section called "Strategies that work." This is a discussion and sample instructional strategies, curricula, and assessments related to the chapter theme that science teachers can use to promote more authentic learning. Finally, there is more on the quote at the beginning of each chapter.

ALTERNATIVE BOOK TITLES THAT I CONSIDERED

In case you are still not clear of what to expect in the remainder of this book, here are a few alternative titles that I considered before settling on the one on the cover:

An inquiry into education, where the rubber meets the road

The complete idiot's guide to not creating a generation of complete idiots

Your child left behind

Race to the top of what?

Solving all of the world's problems through improving science education in order to teach future generations to think and reason intelligently

GRATITUDE

I am indebted to the many wonderful people who supported the work that led to this book. In particular I thank the dedicated principal at the high school in which I taught and his amazing teaching and support staff. I was fortunate to be at such a wonderful school. I am also grateful to CCNY for continuously supporting my work in science education. Most of all, I am grateful to every student with whom I have ever worked who at any point was open to trying to learn or able to teach me. There is no doubt that they are the reason that I love what I do.

With respect to the writing of this book, I am grateful to many friends and colleagues for discussions, suggestions, feedback, constructive criticism, and other support. These include Greg Borman, Sebastien Cormier, Beverly Falk, Adiel Fernandez, Joel Gersten, David Hammer, Takoa Lawson, Federica Raia, Joe Redish, Issa Salame, Waylon Smith, Ken Tobin, my parents, and my two sons. Most of all. I thank my wonderful wife Liz for her unending support and encouragement on this book and for everything else in my life.

PART I

SETTING THE STAGE

A motivating summer experience

THE SUN GOES AROUND THE EARTH

Goals of science education[1]

Since the mass of pupils are never going to become scientific specialists, it is much more important that they should get some insight what scientific method means than they should copy at long range and second hand the results that scientific men have reached. Students will not go so far, perhaps, in the 'ground covered,' but they will be sure and intelligent as far as they do go. And it is safe to say that the few who do go on to be scientific experts will have a better preparation than if they had been swamped by a large mass of purely technical and symbolically stated information. In fact, those that do become successful [in] science are those who by their own power manage to avoid the pitfalls of a traditional scholastic introduction into it.[2]

- John Dewey

JULY 31: TEACHING IN THE SUMMER SCHOLARS PROGRAM

July 31 was near the end of the Summer Scholars Program, my last activity at the college before going off to my sabbatical teaching assignment in the high school. All of my students were so enthusiastic and engaged. This was a real turn of events from the beginning of the summer. The students were experiencing a very different learning experience and by the end of July genuinely enjoyed it. They also recognized the contrast of the program with the way they typically learned science in their schools.

Every summer for the previous seven years, I taught in this program at City College of New York. It is for students from New York City who just finished anywhere from ninth through eleventh grades. The program is academically selective. Admissions requirements vary slightly from year to year but include a minimum of a B average and a letter of recommendation from the guidance office. Many of the students are from specialized high schools. Most are academically very successful. All have elected to spend their summers studying science.

---

[1] The research presented in this chapter and the assessment of results are described and documented in detail at: Steinberg, R. N., Cormier, S., & Fernandez, A. (2009). Probing student understanding of scientific thinking in the context of introductory astrophysics. *Phys. Rev. ST Phys. Educ. Res., 5,* 020104.

[2] Dewey, J. (1916). *Democracy and education.* New York: The Free Press.

3

Like other summers, there were about 20 students in the science cohort. They met 4 days per week for 6 weeks starting right after their high school year ended. A total of 4.5 hours per day was formal class time divided equally between a chemistry class and an astronomy class. Both were delivered in the same spirit. The astronomy class was mine.

Curriculum and instruction were not predicated on covering a prescribed body of information or teaching towards a standardized test. We took this as an opportunity to focus on the scientific process. We focused on depth of understanding of an accessible scope of content. This is in contrast to typical high school science instruction in New York City – and most other places. The contrast resulted in a great culture shock for the students. In school they were accustomed to (and skilled at) succeeding on curriculum and assessment which focuses on memorized facts, prescriptive problem solving, and multiple choice / short answer exams. This class was different, very different.

Observational astronomy is a rich context to exercise student thinking about science. How do you know that the moon goes around the earth or that the earth goes around the sun?[3] How is it that some of those bright dots in the sky (*all of* which seem to revolve around the earth daily) are distant stars but others are planets going around the sun?[4] Models of the universe are not developed simply or directly from observations. They need to be reasoned inferentially from extensive observations, integrating multiple domains of mathematics and physics. It is one thing to state the answers to these questions. It is something very different to be able to understand the nature of science and scientific thinking that underlies how one comes to know the answers. In my astronomy class, students were not told the answers to these questions. They had to answer them on their own.

Due to the nature of the program and the dispositions of the instructors, classroom atmosphere was comfortable and open. Students were encouraged to question, challenge, discuss, and have fun. Nevertheless, the majority of students began the summer clearly out of their comfort zone. They needed to be given a great deal of prodding to provide reasoning, to negotiate what they were doing with each other, and to defend the arguments they made. They readily admitted to seeing a science lesson as a body of information to be provided and written down. They were surprised that we prodded them into figuring things out for themselves instead of just telling them answers. Of course we were there to help them and guide them, but not to do it for them.

As the summer progressed, most students grew increasingly comfortable with the nature of the class. Their skills with working with each other to answer their own questions increased. After repeated practice, they learned the difference between knowing something because they had been told it to be true and knowing something because they understood (and had often executed) the steps

---

[3] From observation, it looks very much like the sun goes around the earth each day.

[4] In a given day, planets appear to move nearly identically to stars. One certainly does not "see" them go around the sun. The leap to the conclusion that planets go around the sun is a big one.

that underlie the idea. By the end of the summer such practices were largely self-directed, typically with pride and self-awareness.

"PROVIDE A COMPLETE SCIENTIFIC ARGUMENT"

Early in the first day of the program, even before the course was defined, the question shown in Figure 1.1 was given. Students answered the question independently and were given all the time they needed. They were in an unfamiliar academic program with new classmates. All indications were that they tried their best to answer the question. This identical question was also given at the end of the program.

Which of the following do you think best approximates the relative motion of the earth and the sun?

A. The sun goes around the earth.

B. The earth goes around the sun.

C. Neither A nor B are correct.

D. I do not know.

As best as you can, provide a proper and complete scientific argument for your answer.

Figure 1.1. Question asked of all students at the beginning and end of the summer program.

More than 90% of the students selected choice B on that first day. This was just like every summer. Choice B reflects agreement with the scientific community. However, there is more to the story when you look at the reasoning they used.

Zhi wrote as a scientific argument "The earth goes around the sun because of many reasons. One is the amount of time and days it takes for the earth to go around the sun. Another reason to account for this is the cycling of seasons we have in each year. This is why the earth goes around the sun." Zhi wrote clearly and in full sentences. He made accurate references to relevant material. In a typical high school class his response likely would have resulted in a reasonable score and positive feedback. The problem is it does not address scientific justification for answering that the earth goes around the sun at all. Referring to the time it takes the earth to go around the sun as a reason that the earth goes around the sun is circular at best. The seasons can be accounted for in the geocentric and the heliocentric model equally well, so citing seasons as scientific justification for the earth going around the sun has no merit.

The scientific argument that Firoza provided was "According to Copernicus's geocentric theory the earth goes around the sun. Also the change of night and day shows that the earth takes different positions and revolves around. Sun setting and sun rising also changes our view of the sun as we travel around it." As with Zhi, this is reasonably well written but without any substance. Like many students, Firoza referred to authority (Copernicus) and jargon (regardless of her choice of "geocentric" instead of "heliocentric"), neither of which constitute scientific justification. The rest of her answer demonstrates a lack of understanding of the relevant ideas as night and day have nothing to do with the conventional description of the revolution of the earth around the sun.

Almost all other student answers also demonstrated a complete lack of any substantive scientific reasoning.

During class, immediately after the written responses were collected, there was a whole class discussion. Student agreement that the earth goes around the sun (choice B) is the right answer was overwhelming. Many prefaced the choice with "of course" and "everyone knows." Explanations matched those written on the pretest such as those of Zhi and Firoza, even as students were given opportunity and encouragement to elaborate.

When my questions revealed holes in their explanations, students asked questions like "Is it the seasons?" or "Does it have to do with the planets?" and then waited for an authoritarian yes or no from me, which never came.

Me: *Could the earth going around the sun cause seasons?*

Jae: *Yes.* (True.)

Me: *Could the sun going around the earth cause seasons?*

Jae: *Yes.* (Hesitantly, but true.)

Me: *Are there seasons?*

Jae: *Yes.*

Me: *What do we know about whether the earth goes around the sun or the sun goes around the earth from seasons?*

Jae: *I don't know* (which is different than "I can't know"... it is unclear which the student intended).

This discussion was a prelude to the substance and philosophy of the summer program. With respect to the exchange about the seasons, the class analyzed the logic of: "If Jane smokes, it will cause her to cough. Jane is coughing. Jane must be a smoker." They articulated to each other whether they agreed or disagreed with this argument and explained their reasoning. They related what they learned about Jane's coughing to the argument about the seasons. Eventually they were able to state clearly why the existence of the seasons does not provide any justification as to whether the earth goes around the sun or the sun goes around the earth.

The students were eager to have the answer to the seemingly simple question about the relative motion of the sun and the earth given directly to them. This was not done at any point during the summer.

INSTRUCTION

Both the instructional philosophy and curriculum employed were largely from the Astronomy modules of *Physics by Inquiry.*[5] Subject matter included daily motion of the sun, size and shape of the earth, phases of the moon, daily and annual motion of the stars, and motion of the planets.

Throughout, the emphasis was on the process of science rather than the presentation of facts. Students actively made observations and used these observations to develop multiple scientific models of the universe. Students made shadow plots of the sun. They experimented with a flashlight and nail and reasoned that they can account for the daily apparent motion of the sun by moving the flashlight or by moving the nail.

After making and sharing observations of the moon, students observed the appearance of a ball near an illuminated bulb in an otherwise dark room. As before, students experimented and reasoned. They came to recognize that they can account for all of their observations of the moon either by thinking of the earth rotating while the sun is stationary or by thinking of the sun and moon going around a stationary earth.[6]

With some help, students observed that the angle between the semicircular phased moon and the sun is indistinguishable from 90°. They then maneuvered the moon ball and sun bulb until they saw the semicircular moon and thought about the angle between the "sun" and "moon" in the model for an observer on the "earth." They literally had to walk all the way across the room from the bulb with the ball in hand before they were able to get the angle even close to their liking. They realized for themselves that the only way the angle between the sun and semicircular moon can be 90° is if the sun is much, much further from the earth than the moon. They were able to articulate exactly how they know the relative distance of the sun and moon from the earth. They reasoned for themselves what they can conclude about the relative size of sun and the moon, given that they appear about the same size in the sky but the sun is way farther away from the earth than the moon.

Daily motion of the stars and planets were explored in a similar manner, with similar results.[7] This process continued with an analysis of the sun, stars, and planets over many months.[8]

---

[5]   McDermott, L. C., & the Physics Education Group at the University of Washington. (1996). *Physics by inquiry.* New York: John Wiley & Sons, Inc..

[6]   If one thinks of the sun going around the earth daily, then the moon is going around the earth daily as well, although at a slightly different rate.

[7]   If one thinks of the sun going around the earth daily, then the stars and planets are also going around the earth daily, but not quite in the same way.

Students learned about the astronomy, how they know about the astronomy, and how to articulate their scientific reasoning. All summer, they were not given answers. Instead they were guided to develop ways in which they could account for their observations. They were constantly asked to justify, explain, reason, and interpret. Given the unanswered question from the pretest, early in the program students repeatedly asked what the right answer was. As the summer went though, there was a shift towards them wanting to answer the question for themselves.

In addition to the observational astronomy, we covered Newton's Laws of motion in a similar inquiry-based spirit. Included was a development of an understanding of gravity and the relationship between force and motion for circular motion. Near the end of the course, but prior to the post-test described below, we covered important relevant historical observations such as phases of the planets and the moons of Jupiter. Implications of these observations and Newton's Laws were alluded to, but still not stated outright. Students were guided to making relevant connections to how we know the earth goes around the sun.[9]

"PROVIDE A COMPLETE SCIENTIFIC ARGUMENT" TAKE 2

At the end of the summer, the identical question shown in Figure 1.1 was asked. The *reasoning* of the student responses to the question both at the beginning of the program and at the end of the program were evaluated with the rubric described at the end of this chapter. On a 5 point scale with 5 being the best reasoning, the average rubric score at the beginning of the program was 1.4.[10] The average rubric score at the end of the program was 3.9. Figures 1.2 and 1.3 show two typical student responses along with the rubric scores.

Like many students, Venkat started the summer with a combination of authoritarian statements and circular reasoning to support his choice of B. (See Figure 1.2.) By the end of the summer, he still answered that the earth goes around the sun. However, he now recognized that the basic observations can be accounted for in either the heliocentric or geocentric model. To support that the earth goes around the sun as the better choice, he integrated Newton's laws and appropriate, more subtle observations of Mars.

Hariti also selected choice B at the beginning of the summer. (See Figure 1.3.) Hariti's support for this choice is difficult to follow. It is based on irrelevant and incorrect observations and reasoning. Her response reflects many students' written and later spoken justifications which were convoluted yet stated confidently. By the end of the summer, Hariti changed her answer to choice D, "I do not know." Regardless, in contrast to her pretest response, her reasoning was much stronger and more clearly developed. She properly justified her choice (regardless of

---

[8] The vast majority of observations of the sun, stars, and planets over many months can be equally well accounted for in either the heliocentric or geocentric models.

[9] Newton's laws and detailed observations of the planets can delineate between the heliocentric and geocentric models of the universe, unlike simple observations of the sun, moon, stars, and seasons.

[10] Data and examples throughout this chapter are from multiple years.

whether it is the answer considered correct) by noting how it is possible to account for her observations in either model of the earth and the sun.

Venkat response at beginning of program:

Choice B, "We know that sun is stationary and does not move. But, earth moves and is not stationary. Also by looking at the Heliocentric Theory, we know that earth revolves around the sun and that's how we get our years." (rubric score 1)

Venkat response at end of program:

Choice B, "Before Newton's Laws were introduced, both A and B would have been possible. If A were the case, then the sun would move clockwise around the earth, and if B were the case then the earth would move counterclockwise around the sun. Both would account for the same conditions. However Newton explained that the more mass an object has the more gravitational pull. From our observations the earth has less mass than the sun, so the gravitational pull is greater. Also we discussed Mars coming closer and the only way that could be accounted for is if the earth and Mars orbits around the sun, and as they orbit the distance between them changes. The laws of motion and force support that the earth goes around the sun." (rubric score 4)

Figure 1.2. Sample verbatim responses to question shown in Figure 1.1.

Hariti response at beginning of program:

Choice B, "The earth goes around the sun because the different hemispheres of the earth receive the sun at different angles at different times of the day. The sun, however is always in the same position when it is visible. Therefore, the sun does not change position, rather, the earth does." (rubric score 1)

Hariti response at end of program:

Choice D, "The relative motion of the earth and the sun can be accounted for in both ways. Through observation. I saw both ways to be accurate. I saw that the earth can go around the sun counter clockwise and account for the relative motion of the sun and the earth. I also saw that the sun can go around the earth clockwise and it still would account for the relative motion of the sun and earth. There is no reason to choose another model using only the sun and earth's relative motion. Therefore, I do not know which model is better because with this information, the results are reproduced with the same amount of accuracy." (rubric score 5)

Figure 1.3. Sample verbatim responses to question shown in Figure 1.1.

Figures 1.2 and 1.3 refer to scientific justification and reasoning. Also of note is the percentage of students who selected each of the choices A through D in Figure 1.1. Prior to instruction, 93% selected choice B. At the end of the program, 52%

selected choice B and 43% selected choice D. One can interpret this as instruction having the opposite effect of improving success since many students switched from the "right" answer to "I do not know." Instead, this result highlights the limitation of multiple choice questions which emphasize recall. Correct responses at the beginning masked student lack of understanding of underlying scientific thinking. Explained "I do not know" responses at the end revealed student insight into well-developed scientific reasoning. In other words, the multiple choice response was not a reflection of student knowledge of science or astronomy.

The split responses between A and D on the post-test are consistent with the instructional approach of having students figure out scientific ideas for themselves. Students were given opportunities to make observations and build scientific models. While support and guidance were provided, answers were not stated authoritatively at any point. In the end, roughly half of the students were convinced that there is sufficient evidence to support that the earth goes around the sun. They justified their answers accordingly. The rest of the students remained unconvinced (even though they were well aware of the "right" answer) and appropriately explained why. Either way, student responses reflected their own thinking and are connected to legitimate scientific reasoning in contrast to parroted, non-understood answers.

"PROVIDE A COMPLETE SCIENTIFIC ARGUMENT" TAKE 3

In addition to being asked to provide a scientific argument about the relative motion of the earth and sun at the end of the summer, students were asked the question about black holes shown in Figure 1.4. The earth-sun question addressed material explicitly covered in the program, even though the question was not answered directly. The black hole question addressed material not at all covered in the program.

Which of the following is most accurate?

A. There are things in the universe called black holes from which not even light can escape.

B. While the expression "black hole" is popular in science fiction, it is not something that really exists.

C. Neither A nor B are correct.

D. I do not know.

As best as you can, provide a proper and complete scientific argument for your answer.

Figure 1.4. Question asked of all students at the end of the summer program. Black holes were not covered.

Most of the students (95%) selected choice D, "I do not know." To gauge student scientific arguments, we developed a rubric similar to the earth-sun one. The average score using this rubric was 3.9, similar to the average score on the earth-sun post-test.

Many of the quotes on the black hole post-test reflect the approach to science emphasized in the program. Juanita wrote "I have absolutely no idea whether black holes exist or not. I have heard of them mentioned, but I never really learned about them, so I really don't know..." Patricia wrote "... Since it isn't something I learned based on observations or experiments, I can only say that 'I do not know' unless I wish to spit out information I don't fully understand." Many were more explicit about referring to what they had learned in class such as Swatti who wrote "If I hadn't taken this class I would have said A, but now I know that I don't have anything to justify that other than 'I read it in a book.'"

The scientific arguments of Juanita, Patricia, and Swatti reflect a strong perspective of the origin of scientific knowledge. However, since they all selected choice D it also represents a potential limitation of their learning science content after having participated in this program. We certainly want our students to have an understanding of science which extends beyond what is constructed from first principles and personal observations. To reach higher levels of understanding of science, students need to be able to recognize how scientific ideas are constructed, when they are able to construct those ideas for themselves, and when they should accept the findings of others having gone through similar steps properly.

WHO CARES ABOUT ASTRONOMY?

The entire astronomy course was built around exploring the relative motion of the earth and the sun. Students got to participate in the process of science, develop their reasoning skills, and negotiate conflicting arguments. These and many other important skills are transferable to so many domains in and out of science. All of these skills are best developed when practiced in a real context. Students also learned science content. Observational astronomy just happened to the context.

There are so many other topics with which this could be done. For example, the complementary chemistry course in the Summer Scholars Program, taught by my colleagues Issa Salame and Takoa Lawson, followed the same strategies of the astronomy course. However, in that course they explored how we know about the nature of the atom. What are the specific observations and experiments that have led to the understanding of atomic structure? Are there multiple ways to account for our observations? What is the nature of scientific models in atomic physics?

In previous years, I taught with the same spirit but the topic was introductory quantum mechanics. Students started with simple observations of light bulbs, shadows, water tanks, and long springs. They built on their own observations and reasoning until they understood electron diffraction and the probabilistic interpretation of subatomic particles. Alternatively I have had students follow a similar path from thrown balls, emitted sound , and illuminated light on moving trains to Einstein's Theory of Relativity.

The best context in which to teach science in this spirit though might be the theory of evolution. What evidence is there that points to the age of the earth? (And what does that have to do with anything?) What are our observations of similar but different species and the environments in which they live? What can we learn from fossils? How do we know about genetics and how do we relate this to the theory of evolution? What experiments can we examine today that relate to the theory of evolution?

Scientific literacy ties at least as much to an understanding of the process and reasoning of science as it does to the body of information that is known. And there are so many wonderful contexts in which the students can engage to learn it all simultaneously.

REFLECTIONS ON UNDERSTANDING SCIENCE AND GOALS OF SCIENCE EDUCATION

In addition to the often discussed and detailed need for understanding specific scientific content, one of the goals of science education needs to be that students should be able to think and reason scientifically. The results presented in this chapter, from a dedicated and academically successful population, indicate that we are failing to meet this goal. After traditional instruction, even this privileged group struggles with basic understandings about the nature of scientific thinking. I have administered the same instruction and questions with thousands of other pre-college students, K-12 teachers, and college science students from all over the country. The results are fundamentally the same every time.

There is a need to look into what is happening in schools and explore how it comes to be this way. What is it that is going on in science classes that leaves the best students unable to give reasons that the earth goes around the sun, or even understand what it means to give a reason?

Faulty approaches to learning and knowing science are the norm. Faulty approaches to learning and knowing in general are also the norm. But I firmly believe that this can change. When given the opportunity to participate in the process of learning, students can succeed, and they embrace the opportunity. The Summer Scholars Program convinced me of this.

If the question in Figure 1.1 were a standardized test question, the 93% "correct" response rate would be interpreted as high success. Students and instructors would be lauded. There would be a march to more advanced material where it would be inevitable that students would have an even harder time understanding the nature of science and the underlying concepts and reasoning. They would therefore revert further into a strategy of memorize and repeat. Only after some probing does it become clear that student understanding is inadequate. Even if this probing is more challenging than a typical standardized test can accomplish, it is important if we are to emphasize a meaningful understanding of science.

Educators of science, as well as all other disciplines, need to prioritize the best interests of students regardless of the system in which we teach. We should identify that which is of value in the way our students are assessed and work towards them having success on these assessments. I certainly prefer that students recognize the community consensus about the relative motion of the earth and the sun, but this need be in conjunction with understanding why it is the community consensus.

Educators of science, as well as all other disciplines, need to redirect the system to one which results in education of our children that is of most value. What is successful in the Summer Scholars Program can and does work.

JOHN DEWEY

John Dewey published the words at the beginning of this chapter in 1916. I first learned of the significance of Dewey and his educational philosophies as a graduate student at Yale. I still remember how much sense he made to me then. I look at these words today and they make even more sense now. Fleeting collections of non-understood statements coupled with a perspective that learning means being told is of so little value. Learning how to think and reason scientifically by actually doing science is a much better idea. This is regardless of the breadth of content covered. This is regardless of whether the student will eventually be going on to a career in science. However, I can't help but fear that these words of Dewey are not being given the attention they deserve.

RATING STUDENT REASONING ON THE EARTH-SUN QUESTION

Table 1 describes the rubric used to score student responses to the scientific argument question of Figure 1.1. The answers are verbatim and representative. "Pre" and "Post" refer to whether the response was given prior to or after instruction. A, B, C, and D refer to the multiple choice response given to the question.

Table 1. Rubric used to score student reasoning for earth-sun question.

Rubric Score	Description	Sample answers
1	Students use jargon, authority, circular reasoning, or irrelevant observations / experiments and it represents a significant part of their answer.	Pre, B "Copernicus's heliocentric theory proves that the sun is the center of the solar system and all contained celestial bodies orbit around it." Pre, B "The sun is the center of our solar system. All nine planets revolve around this star. We know that the earth revolves around the sun because we have night on one side of the earth, and day on the other. The changing of the seasons is also a result of the earth revolution." Pre, B "The earth turns on its own axis while following an elliptical orbit around the sun in which at some points it is closer or further from the sun. This full path around the sun is the duration of one year. The sun also spinning."
2	Student cites relevant observations / experiments in support of their choice, thoughts are not clearly connected, little or incorrect development of ideas or reasoning, no distinction between models.	Pre, B "I believe the sun has greater gravitational force than the earth does. So the sun pulls in the earth and the earth has no chance to move around the sun" Pre, B "The earth goes around the sun because the sun has a greater gravitational pull than the earth does. Therefore, rather than the sun being pulled into the earth's orbit, the earth and the rest of the 9 planets get pulled into the sun's orbit"
3	Student refers to relevant observations / experiments but part of explanation is erroneous or problematic OR student recognizes an inability to answer to the question.	Pre, D "I don't know, in some classes you are informed the earth goes around the sun, proof by scientific observation (through change of seasons, shadows of grounded object etc), however, like all scientific theories, you never know if it is true all the time (someone can always find another plot to say it is wrong). People used to think the sun goes around the earth, so I really don't know what's the true answer of this question." Post, B "The earth goes around the sun because from the observations I made about the other planets going around the sun. The planets are much smaller than the sun so they revolve around the sun. According to Newton's law $F=ma$ and smaller things revolve around bigger things. Since the force between the sun and the earth is the same and the mass are very different. It means that the earth will have a lot more acceleration than the sun since earth is little compared to the sun"

4	Student cites observations / experiments distinguishing between models in a consistent way but explanation is not developed or is incomplete.	Post, A "We can perfectly account for all our observations w/ this model: seasons, phases of the moon, planets going around and moving backwards and forwards etc. but there is one characteristic that shows that this is the best choice: WE DON'T MOVE! Although proponents of the alternative view say that this model is so complicated and will get less migraines, they still not been able to explain why we don't feel ourselves moving. Also, just because it's complicated doesn't mean it's wrong, we must accept what is there is not a fantasy that is easier. The sun goes around the earth, no doubt about that."
5	Student cites observations / experiments distinguishing between 2 models and supports choice with proper explanation relevant to their answer (regardless of multiple choice response).	Post, B "Based on our observations, we can account for the daily motion of the sun, stars, and planets using both models (geocentric & heliocentric). If we strictly rely on this as far as we can tell we do not know. Using our knowledge of physics, we may find evidence that gives the heliocentric model preference over the geocentric model. We know that the size of the sun is much greater than the size of the earth. (The distance between the moon and the earth is much greater than the size of the earth and in pt 1 we showed that the distance between the sun and the earth is much greater than that, but yet the sun appears to be the same size as the moon in the sky therefore the size of the sun is much greater than that of the moon and of the earth) By Newton's 3rd law the force that the sun exerts on the earth is the same exact force, opposite, with the same magnitude that the earth applies on the sun. In order to maintain circular motion, at as constant speed, k, the direction of the force must be towards the center of the circle (earth/sun). If the geocentric model was true, the acceleration that the earth has must be much less than that of the sun. This implies that the earth's mass is much greater than the sun so the sun can orbit around earth. However we know that the $m\_earth < M\_sun$. So the earth revolves around the sun" Post, D "The relative motion of the earth and the sun can be accounted for in both ways. Through ray observation. I saw both ways to be accurate. I saw that the earth can go around the sun counter clockwise and account for the relative motion of the sun and the earth. I also saw that the sun can go around the earth clockwise and it still would account for the relative motion of the sun and earth. There is no reason to choose another model using only the sun and earth's relative motion. Therefore, I do not know which model is better because with this information, the results are reproduced with the same amount of accuracy."

15

AWAY FROM THE IVORY TOWER

Inquiry

In theory there is no difference between theory and practice. In practice there is. [1]

- Yogi Berra

AUGUST 15: A CHANGE IN CONTEXT

With hopes of following up on my experience in the Summer Scholars Program, I accepted a position as a full time science teacher in Urban High School (UHS)[2] in New York City. I knew that most of the students would be different than those in the Summer Scholars Program. I knew that the environment and expectations would be different. I knew that there would be so much for me to learn. As I went through my orientations in August leading up to teaching at UHS, I was eager, hopeful, excited, and more than a little nervous.

Prior to my sabbatical, from my experiences learning physics I saw the beauty and elegance of the subject matter, often delivered to me by master physicists. From my experiences in education I saw the importance of setting up an environment, both affectively and cognitively, conducive to maximizing learning. From my experiences conducting science education research I saw the need to understand and address specific difficulties students have learning the subject matter. From my experience at orientation at UHS on August 15, I learned that all my other experiences meant nothing compared to getting through the day unscathed (sometimes literally). I also quickly learned that all that mattered to the school was my students' success on a standardized test that I was confident correlated little with anything that was important about knowing physics.

It was clear that teachers are taught one way, are taught to teach it another, and are told something different still by the school system. We are then put in a room where none of it works. First year teachers quickly recognize that classroom management is a big part of the challenge, but not the only one.

My experience was in a poor community in New York City. Almost all of the students were Black or Hispanic and from modest means. In this particular school

---

[1] Although this quote is often attributed to Yogi Berra, it is not clear who the original author of these words is. Regardless, this is typical of the kind of thing that Yogi Berra would say.

[2] Urban High School is a fictitious name I use for the school in which I taught. I was tempted to use "School of Sabbatical" since the acronym would have felt more appropriate, but went with the simpler UHS anyway.

there was strong leadership and good support services. There were fewer than 25 students assigned in each of my classes. A relatively large proportion of the students from UHS go to college. However, those that know more than me about the New York City school system told me that student background, student discipline, and overall challenges at UHS are not very different from what is encountered in many New York City public schools. This particular school encourages students to take physics though, which allowed me to have a full cross section of students. It also presented the challenge that many of them would not be motivated or interested in taking the course.

During that last month of August, before classes started, I thought a great deal about both my motivations for wanting to teach at UHS and in the very challenging context in which I was about to be immersed. I aspired to build on what I did in the Summer Scholars Program, but there was more to it than that.

MOTIVATION 1: WORK WITH COLLEGE PHYSICS STUDENTS

There were many motivations for wanting to teach in (and understand) a New York City high school. One came from my teaching college physics. Most of my CCNY students are in the School of Engineering. They are largely graduates of New York City high schools. Practically speaking, they represent the higher performing, more motivated, better prepared of the high school graduates. Like many physics professors (at CCNY and elsewhere) I am often disappointed at the overall preparedness of these students for legitimate college level work. Many do not survive the introductory course. They are subsequently not eligible for careers in science or engineering.

Along with Joel Gersten, my colleague in the Physics Department, we administered a baseline diagnostic test for incoming engineering students taking physics.[3] By any reasonable expectation, the questions should have been solvable by this group. Questions were like:

A gallon of gas costs $1.20. How much gas can I get for $1.00?

Solve: $\dfrac{x}{2} = \dfrac{3x}{4} + 1$

We are growing a population of bacteria in a jar. At 11:00 a.m. there is one bacterium in the jar. The bacteria divide once every minute so that the population doubles every minute. At 12:00 noon the jar is full. At what time was the jar half full?

---

[3] Many of the questions we used were taken from or based on the *Diagnostic Test of Basic Skills* by Jerome Epstein.

18

Students averaged less than a 70% on the diagnostic. Fewer than half got the question above about the bacteria correct.[4] Results of the diagnostic and many other measures of student readiness are conclusive. Too many students are coming to college with insufficient math (and literacy) aptitude. Their ability to perform high school level math skills is poor. Their ability to transfer these skills to unfamiliar contexts is even worse.

When teaching college physics, I find weak math skills to be a problem, but I find student approaches to learning an even greater problem. When working on a homework assignment, the strategy that students use is to find a nearly identical solved question as a model to copy from. If one is not available, they look for a formula with a collection of variables that looks similar, regardless of whether the formula is relevant. These are not effective strategies for learning physics. These are not useful strategies for success outside of a physics classroom. I would rather listen to a student rub her fingernails against a blackboard than watch her do physics like this.

When learning the material, rarely do I see a student identify the big idea, try to relate the situation to the real world, or integrate conceptual understanding to problem solving. I believe that student math skill weaknesses are easier to overcome than these flawed approaches.

One of the standard problems that I assign in introductory physics is:

A 10 kg piece of zinc at 71°C is placed in a container of water. The water has a mass of 20 kg and a temperature of 10°C before the zinc is added. What is the final temperature of the water and zinc?

This problem can be solved using some involved, but still high school level algebra. Mark was a good student in one of my introductory physics classes. He was intelligent and routinely submitted homework, prepared for exams, and cared about his grades. For the most part, he even set up the mathematics of this particular problem correctly. However, like so many other students, Mark did not calculate the right value for the final temperature. He came up with 3°C.

Here is a college student who left high school without reasonable mastery of high school algebra. Regardless, somehow, Mark was comfortable with (blind to?) a 71°C piece of Zinc combined with 10°C water resulting in a final temperature of 3°C. He did not have an approach to problem solving where he tried to relate his calculated result to what makes reasonable sense. He presented an answer for the final temperature of the two substances which was not between the two initial temperatures. He should have seen this nonsensical outcome as a clue that something was wrong and gone back to check his work. He did not.

Most of my students are not coming to college with the skill sets they need. When resolving vector force components, they could only do the trigonometry when the forces are parallel to one of the edges of the paper. They struggle with

---

[4] One minute earlier.

electrostatics problems because they only know algebra if the symbol "x" is the unknown. They report the mass of a swinging pendulum to be more than the mass of the sun. They do not think to start with the big idea that the initial and final energies of a system must be the same unless told explicitly to do so. Ohm's law is applied even if there is an open circuit and no path for the current to go. Students like Mark should come to college with mastery of high school mathematics, strong problem solving strategies, and a disposition to make sense of what they are doing as they go. They come with none of this.

Therefore, one motivating question that I had going into the high school was what could I learn that will make me a more informed college physics professor?

MOTIVATION 2: WORK WITH SCIENCE TEACHERS

Another motivation for wanting to teach in (and understand) a New York City high school came from my role as Program Director of Science Education at CCNY. In many different capacities I work with, teach courses for, and advise New York City science teachers. I am pretty sure in my understanding of the subject matter, of the nature of science, of pedagogical strategies, and of how students learn. I am completely sure that this is not enough.

I routinely hear from teachers in the program that what they learn in my courses is wonderful and that it reflects the way that science classes should be taught. They appreciate learning science the same way that the Summer Scholars students do. They enthusiastically see the value when reflecting on the process. They appreciate having the opportunity to analyze how their students do and do not learn real science. Nevertheless, they tell me that it is all irrelevant because that is not the way the schools work. "That won't help prepare them for the state tests." "Kids can't do that." "It's all about classroom management."

There seems to be an understanding of the right way to teach the content, skills, reasoning, and processes of science but that it is irrelevant to what goes on in real science classrooms. There is something very wrong with this picture.

Therefore, another motivating question that I had going into the high school was what could I learn that will make me more effective when working with science teachers?

INQUIRY INTO INQUIRY

In preparation for my sabbatical, I spent the previous year participating in an alternative teacher certification program. I continued in the program through my year teaching at UHS. I'd like to say that I was motivated to do this to maximize my ability to succeed as a teacher. However, the truth is that I did this because I was not permitted to teach in a public school without the proper certification. As a result, I took the courses (several of which I had previously taught) needed to obtain the right credentials.

Classes were daily in the summer and one evening each week during the school year. I did all of the required class work, projects, and homework assignments. I did my field work, where I visited a wide variety of classrooms in multiple schools in the community. In the end, I appreciated the opportunity to learn and to experience what other teachers experience when entering into the teaching profession.

One recurring term in all of the education classes (and later in many professional development sessions that I went to) was "inquiry." However, while so many used the word, there was never clarity in what it meant. Some common associations with inquiry were "hands on," "interactive," and "group work." All of that sounds good to me. One dictionary definition of inquiry is "seeking truth, information, knowledge." I never heard that one in any of the classes that I took, but I like that too. I particularly like the "seeking" part, which is in contrast to just "having" or "being told." Science is inquiry. Learning is inquiry. I guess learning science should be inquiry squared.

To me, what my students did in the Summer Scholars Program exemplified learning by inquiry. I also saw all kinds of other wonderful examples of activities where students were actively constructing their own understanding of all kinds of topics by what looked to me like inquiry learning. Some were in science and others were not. Some were in one period lessons and some were in extensive units. Some were on prescribed curricula selected by the instructor and others were extensive group projects where the students helped define a topic and a research question. It was very exciting and looked very successful.

However, while hands on, interactive, and group work can facilitate learning by inquiry, more often I saw it described when the activities were not what I would call inquiry. Students were not seeking truth, information, or knowledge. They were not making sense of the world, not exploring ideas, not inquiring. Perhaps they were actively engaged with hands on activities by making a model of the solar system with Styrofoam balls. Perhaps they were working in groups to come up with mnemonics to memorize the periodic table. They were not however doing things that led them to understand where knowledge comes from or how it is understood. The teachers claimed to be teaching science by inquiry. Activities like these might serve a function in science classrooms, but students are not learning science by inquiry.

This is not good enough. In the Summer Scholars Program I saw how it was possible to have students build a scientific understanding of the whole universe based on their own investigations, construction, and reasoning. If this could be done for the entire universe, surely it could be done for much smaller things. Things like projectiles, circuits, and atoms. Things like ecosystems, plant life, and cells. Maybe even for things like global warming, nuclear energy, and recycling.

In the Summer Scholars Program I asked the black hole question where students did not have the opportunity to learn that material by inquiry. I had concern with some of their responses. Even when material is introduced by authority and not by inquiry,[5] students need to understand the process of science and the process of inquiry so well that they can identify explicitly reliable knowledge that they have not developed on their own. They also need to understand the kind of inquiry that was done by others to come to that knowledge. Science and inquiry need be understood so well that students can tell whether someone else has done it well, poorly, or not at all. Science and inquiry need to be understood so well that students can identify when they have obtained information without having participated in the process. How can any of this happen if students don't have extensive opportunities to do scientific inquiry themselves?

And if inquiry is really understood, it should also be part of things like politics, religion, society, and more. The science classroom is a great place to learn, develop, and exercise the skills of inquiry. The entire world is a great place to have those skills.

REFLECTIONS ON GOING TO UHS

My preparation for teaching at UHS was a culmination and a beginning, filled with so much excitement. I had worked hard and long in my career trying to understand and affect science education, often concerned about what was happening in classrooms at all levels. Here was a great opportunity to try to learn. What better learning opportunity is there for a science educator than immersion into a setting like this? For me it was inquiry into inquiry where the rubber meets the road. The rest of the book is a reflection on my seeking of truth, information, and knowledge.

STRATEGIES THAT WORK: INQUIRY

It might not be easy to articulate what classroom inquiry is, but I agree with the consensus that it needs to be a focus in education. The astronomy curricula elaborated on in the previous chapter is inquiry. Students given the opportunity to learn this way succeed in learning astronomy. They are learning science. They are learning more. Below are two lessons on other topics which are inquiry in nature. In each case, students construct for themselves an understanding of scientific knowledge and process. They are also learning content specifically identified in many "standards."

The first lesson is on the speed of light. It is intended to be done after an understanding of the heliocentric model of the solar system and an understanding of planetary motion. Before the lesson, there is a whole class discussion on whether light propagation is instantaneous or extremely fast *and* on what specific scientific evidence any answer is based. In the lesson below, students are able to

---

[5] It is obvious that some portion of material that students should know will need to be presented by authority.

integrate their knowledge of mathematics and astronomy to calculate a reasonable estimation of the speed of light.

The second lesson is on the nature electrical interactions and how one comes to understand these interactions.[6,7] This activity is particularly intended as an exercise for science teachers, a lesson in both electrical interactions and pedagogy. Charge, neutral, and polarization have been deliberately replaced by the fictitious words "sharge," "nukral," and "posterization." The purpose for this is to focus on the science of electrical interactions that arise from simple observations and reasoning. Use of the fictitious words preempts attempts to mask a lack of understanding of the concepts with half-understood application of technical jargon.

Lesson on determination of light speed from astronomical observations[8]

The moon of Jupiter Io is observed to appear out of an eclipse every time it orbits Jupiter with a period of 42 hours, 30 minutes (+/- 2 s). One observation of Io emerging from an eclipse is just east of south at 11:44:45 pm on June 28 (+/- 2s).

1. Predict when the moon would come out of the eclipse after 97 more orbits.

2. It is observed that Io comes out of the eclipse 6:36:58 pm December 24 (+/- 2 s) Is this consistent with your prediction? If not, resolve the conflict.

3. Estimate the speed of light. Explain your reasoning

Lesson on the nature of electrical interactions

A. Interactions

Press a piece of tape (about 15-20 cm) firmly on a smooth unpainted surface. Peel the tape off quickly. Describe in your own words the behavior of the tape as you bring objects toward it (e.g. a hand, a pen).

Make another piece of tape as described above. Bring the second piece of tape toward the first. Describe your observations.

How does the distance between the tapes affect the interaction between them? Explain how you know.

---

[6]   This lesson is based on the charge tutorial from *Tutorials in introductory physics*, McDermott, L.C. Shaffer, P.S. and the Physics Education Group at the University of Washington (Prentice Hall, Upper Saddle River NJ, 1998), which also includes many other inquiry-based activities.

[7]   For a description of the research that underlies the Tutorial activities and documentation of their effectiveness, see the published papers cited at: http://www.phys.washington.edu/groups/peg.

[8]   These fabricated data are similar conceptually to early observations of Ole Römer in the 17th century, but are different in detail to make the calculation of the speed of light more accessible to high school students.

CHAPTER 2

Each member of your group should press tape onto the surface and write a "B" (for bottom) on it. Then press another tape on top of each B tape and write "T" (for top) on it. Slowly pull each pair of tapes off the table as a unit. After they are off the table, separate the T and B tapes quickly.

Describe the interactions between the following when they are brought near one another.

- two T tapes

- two B tapes

- a T and a B tape

- a T tape and a small piece of paper

- a B tape and a small piece of paper

- two small pieces of paper

We say that a material is **sharged** if it behaves in the manner that the T tape and the B tape behave. Otherwise we say that the material is **nukral**.

Describe a procedure that you could use to determine if an unknown object is sharged or nukral.

Is nukral a type of sharge? Explain.

Obtain a rod and a cloth. Rub the rod with the cloth and then hold the rod near newly made T and B tapes. Determine whether the rod is sharged or nukral. If it is sharged, determine if it is sharged T or sharged B. Explain specifically how you know.

B. Other Sharges

A person brings to you a material that she claims is sharged, but is a different kind of sharge than both the T tape and the B tape.

Explain how you can determine if the unknown material is in fact sharged.

Explain how you can determine if the unknown material is sharged differently than both the T tape and the B tape.

Is it possible that there are 3 different types of sharge? 4 different types? Explain.

C. Posterization

A small ball is sharged T on one side and equally sharged B on the other side. The ball is placed near a T sharge, as shown to the right.

Would the ball be attracted toward, repelled from, or unaffected by the T sharge? Explain.

Hang a small nukral metal ball from a string. Then bring a sharged rod near the ball without touching it. Describe what you observe.

The situation above suggests a way to think about the interaction between a sharged object and an unsharged object. Use your answer to question 1 above to try to account for your observation in question 2. Draw a sketch showing the sharge distribution on the ball to support your answer.

YOGI BERRA

Some of the greatest minds in history have helped me form and frame my ideas presented in this book, from Plato to Einstein, from Churchill to King. For this chapter I went with a baseball lifer who quit school in eighth grade, someone who seems to always make so little sense but in reality makes such perfect sense: Yogi Berra.[9] To talk about science teaching, learning, standards, and assessments in theory is one thing. In practice, what happens to students (and to teachers) in a real science classroom is not the same. I have spent my entire career trying to understand the best way to teach science and to work with teachers and students of all levels. What can I learn from teaching in today's educational climate in an inner city science lassroom? A lot!

---

[9] Whether or not Yogi Berra was the original author of these words is not important here.

PART II

TEACHING AT UHS

Science education where the rubber meets the road

A DISTANCE OF 24 SECONDS

Epistemology

I do not feel obliged to believe that the same God who has endowed us with senses, reason, and intellect has intended us to forgo their use.

You cannot teach a man anything; you can only help him to find it within himself.

  - Galileo Galilei

SEPTEMBER 4: MY FIRST DAY TEACHING

On my first day at UHS, I was told that there were no more keys to the staff bathroom. It was my first challenge as a new teacher in the school. Students immediately tested me with breaking dress code, texting during class, and using language I never thought that a child would say to an adult. Others were friendly, eager, and wanted to know what brought me to their school. My lesson plans were all ready and I was eager to get started, but with all of the paperwork and with so many students coming and going, nothing really got off the ground. I had so many emotions, but all I could think about all morning was "What am I going to do if I have to go to the bathroom?"

Luckily, with the help of very supportive colleagues, I survived that first day. I even got a black market key to the bathroom before the day was done.

REGENTS PHYSICS AND ME

The majority of my teaching assignment at UHS was the standard high school physics course. In New York State this is called Regents physics. Like most of the subjects covered in high school in New York, Regents physics culminates with a standardized test students call "the Regents."[1] My students were mostly juniors and seniors. They had been through multiple Regents exams spanning all subjects. It wasn't just Regents tests though. These students were all born in the 1990's. They had been through all kinds of testing since grade school. One way or another, enormous value was always placed on the scores that they got on their different tests, including their Regents exams.

---

[1]   Although I write a great deal about the physics Regents in this book, many subjects in many states at many grade levels have some kind of a similar standardized exam at the end of the year.

As indicated in the state core curriculum and the Regents exam, Regents physics covers process, inquiry, lab, and math skills in content areas which include mechanics, energy, electricity and magnetism, optics, waves, and modern physics.[2] Subject matter is advanced, even by the standards that I am used to in college physics. My much more advanced college students struggle with their curricula despite the lesser scope and depth of coverage compared to what is mandated in Regents physics. It is easy for experts to write an ambitious list of what they want high school students to know after taking a year of physics. What they wrote though is not reasonable if real understanding of the material is the goal.

The combination of high stakes testing with ambitious content coverage was intimidating to me as a new teacher in the school. It was at odds with my belief that learning should be deep and meaningful. Teaching at UHS, I was learning that the approaches and expectations that students had developed through many years compounded the conflict.

Despite the challenges, I was determined to make the course one where students had to make real sense of the material as they learned it. In the first few weeks, the subject matter was motion. I avoided problems which encourage students to revert to a strategy of look up a formula and substitute numbers regardless of whether there was understanding of what they were calculating. Instead, I tried to focus on activities where they had to estimate, connect formalism to the real world, know when and how to apply different models, and reflect on whether what they were doing made sense. I believed that understanding the material would serve the students well, even if the Regents questions were of a different nature. If in my attempt to serve my students best I failed to cover the full scope of topics on the Regents, I would deal with that later.

I de-emphasized questions like "Determine the range of a projectile launched with an initial velocity of 25.4 m/s at an angle of 35° above a level surface." These kinds of problems tend to be solved by students algorithmically, without recognition of the big ideas, without a conceptual foundation of velocity or acceleration in 2 dimensions, and without an understanding of where the formulas came from or when they apply.

My goal was high academic standards, and I meant it. Therefore I tried to focus more on questions like "How long would it take a penny to fall to the ground from the top of the Empire State Building?" or "What is a safe distance to drive behind a car on the West Side Highway?" There was no formula or worked model problem that simply provided a solution. These problems took longer, and could not be solved without really understanding so many important ideas of introductory motion. Even though more challenging, I felt that the students had the background knowledge necessary to solve them.

Students had to make estimates, come up with a strategy to solve the problem, know when and how to convert units, understand what the concepts and formulas mean, and work with each other. Assignments reflected these priorities, even though much of each assignment was easier and more traditional. At the time, I

---

[2] www.nysed.gov.

genuinely believed that all of the students had the skill and intelligence to get perfect scores on every question and achieve full understanding. Reflecting back, I believe this even more.

THE CAR TRAVELS A TOTAL DISTANCE OF 24 SECONDS

Tommy was class clown, although I did not find him particularly funny. He was a regular disruption. His politeness and respect made it easier, but he was a disruption nonetheless. As a student, Tommy was not that strong, but he wanted to pass. Even if he did not do well, he was usually serious when he took the exams. He might not have had the right skills or strategies, but he wanted success.

One of Tommy's exams included the following question, similar to what can be expected on a Regents exam:

A car having an initial speed of 16 meters per second is uniformly brought to rest in 4.0 seconds. How far does the car travel during this 4.0 second interval?

After some unintelligible calculations using one of the standard equations (which was not appropriate for this problem), Tommy wrote as an answer "24 seconds." If I had asked Tommy outside of school how far something traveled in 4 seconds, there is no way he would have answered with 24 seconds. Asking him in class was apparently a different story.

A score of zero for this 3 point question seemed too generous, so I gave Tommy a score of "– 1 ½ gallons" out of 3. After class I talked to Tommy about why I scored him the way I did. I was glad that he appeared to get the point. I am also glad that he was amused.

BECAUSE IT SAYS SO ON THE REFERENCE TABLE

One of the important elements of science that I stressed in teaching was how we know what we know. Science is a way of making sense of the world, not just a body of information. Whether a student was doing an independent project or completing a lab, whether I was lecturing on new material or facilitating group work, I emphasized the development of ideas and the process of science. I emphasized inquiry learning.

As part of the required curriculum I covered the propagation of light. I started with asking if light is something that travels from one place to another instantaneously or just extremely fast. I asked the students to try to think of a way to figure out the answer to this question.

Me: *How can we measure the speed of light?*

Amanda: *I know, it's 3.0 x 10^8 m/s.*

The answer was stated incredulously, by Amanda and so many others. Why am I asking such a simple question? The answer is as obvious as knowing that the earth goes around the sun!

Not only was there no idea for how to measure the speed of light, there was no appreciation for the question of how something is determined. Science was something you were told and the reason something was known was because you were told it. There was nothing more to discuss.

I tried to direct my students to what seemed like a reasonable place to start. Imagine two people on separate mountain tops, but within line of sight of each other. They plan an experiment where the first turns on a light and the instant the second sees the light, she turns on her light. The first observer then notes the time it takes before he sees the light arrive at him from the second observer.[3] I figured that this would be a great opportunity to talk about experimentation, speed, reaction time, and measurement uncertainty. I figured it would be a great way to at least begin to think about a way to measure the speed of light. I figured wrong.

Me: *How can we use this experiment to determine the speed of light?*

Bill: *I can get it from the reference table.*

Me: *I want you to know where the value given comes from.*

Bill: *It comes from the reference table.*

The reference table is a table of definitions, symbols, formulas, physical constants, and other such material students are allowed to have with them when taking the Regents. I assume that the hope is that the students will not spend their time memorizing these things. This could cause them to see physics as a collection of definitions, symbols, formulas, physical constants, and other such material to be memorized and repeated. Instead, the students see physics as a collection of definitions, symbols, formulas, physical constants, and other such material to be looked up on the reference table.

Regardless of the reference table, my experience was that students saw all of science as a collection of definitions, symbols, formulas, physical constants, and other such material. This was their approach to my class despite all of my attempts to convince them otherwise. Science by inquiry was foreign to their approach and to their world view.

My lesson about the speed of light took more time than I wanted, but I eventually made my point. It was worth the time.

---

[3] This is conceptually a sound strategy to measure the speed of light. However, it turns out that light is traveling too fast for it to work experimentally. Human reaction time is far greater than light travel time.

MORE THAN REFERENCE TABLES

I informed my students that some of their exams might be open book, a strategy that I often use when teaching in college. This was more than just a reference table. Students could bring their book, their notes, other books, other notes, and whatever else they wanted. Reaction was pretty polarized. Many audibly expressed their satisfaction, believing that all of the answers would be right at their fingertips. The rest of the students were far less jubilant, often speculating aloud that if all that information was right at their fingertips then the questions would probably be very hard.

I do not believe either disposition is relevant. Of course I knew the kinds of questions that I would put on the exams. Students would have to think, reason, and problem solve. I did not prioritize memorizing, particularly that which was not understood. The questions could be easy, hard, or anything else. They would just not be of the nature where repeating jargon or following a prescribed procedure would be the emphasis. I wanted my students to see that intending to use a strategy of looking up answers was not the way to go.

I shared my motives with my students. I told them that I wanted deep and functional understanding. I wanted testing to improve their ability to process, apply, and synthesize more than memorize. I wanted to model the real world where intelligent access to unlimited information is a critical part of problem solving. (What job requires you to perform a task in isolation without being allowed to look anything up?) Students smiled approvingly. Buy-in to my motives and approaches seemed reasonable, but the school year was young.

MR. LOWREY

I got to observe many teachers of many subjects at multiple schools. It was part of my responsibility as a teacher in training. It was one of my obligations of being a teacher in my school.

One of the teachers that I observed was Mr. Lowrey, a physics teacher in a high school in which one had to excel in middle school in order to be admitted. He was an energetic, young Ivy League graduate who had been teaching high school for about the last five years. He was bright, professional, and pleasant to talk to. He was rated highly in his school and his students' success on the Regents was strong.[4] I was eager to observe one of his classes and discuss physics teaching with him.

I arrived at Mr. Lowrey's class before most of the students. The "Do Now" was posted and students went straight to work on it. The Do Now task was to search the internet for the definition of inertia. Students went right to work on it with each seeming to know exactly what Mr. Lowrey wanted. There was a computer at each student station. As students found definitions online, the definition and the student

---

[4] Clearly the best way to get your students to excel on a test is to start with students most likely to excel on the test. (Mr. Lowrey's school selected for students based on academic success in middle school.)

name were posted real time via a computer projector at the front of the room. Inertia:

A property of matter by which it remains at rest or in uniform motion in the same straight line unless acted upon by some external force.

The resistance an object has to a change in its state of motion.

An object at rest tends to stay at rest and an object in motion tends to stay in motion with the same speed and in the same direction unless acted upon by an unbalanced force.

After about 5 minutes, Mr. Lowrey pressed those who had not posted to do so. (He had the technology and authority and used both.) He then reviewed the postings and noted how they did in fact represent descriptions of inertia.

Using the same computer projector, Mr. Lowrey then presented the definitions of force, net force, equilibrium, normal force, and other related terms in a beautifully prepared PowerPoint presentation. Weight was presented as $W = mg$ and this was described and applied.

A worksheet was then distributed and completed where students had to read text and integrate the words that they had been defining. There was fill in the blank. For example, "Gravity is the force of _____ between_____ _____." (The correct answers from the list of words were "attraction," "all," and "masses.") There was complete the table. (For example "weight" went with "caused by the pull of gravity.") Students calculated the weight when given the mass and mass when given the weight.

I thought about how Mr. Lowrey would be reviewed by an administrator. He managed the class skillfully and was a clear authority in front of the room. Check. He had his students engaged (at least in one sense of the word). Check. Students did their Do Now, test prep, literacy, and calculations, all on state mandated curriculum. Check, check, check, and check. He used technology in a most impressive way. Double check.

Then I thought about the extent to which Mr. Lowrey was preparing his students to be successful on the Regents. Students were "learning" the words and formulas that they needed to know. They were practicing applying them and doing the calculations. I even spoke to Mr. Lowrey later about the Regents and he noted that he had them practice many Regents exams at the beginning of the year before going through the curricula. He said that gave them a window of what they were going to need to know to succeed. He said that it would prepare them to focus in what they needed to learn. I think he was right and his results bore him out.

Next I thought about the development of student thinking about scientific ideas and reasoning skills. Inertia is a difficult concept with which my college students routinely struggle. They might "know" the word, but typically have no sense of its meaning or application. It is certain that even if Mr. Lowrey's students were able to repeat the definition from the internet, they were unlikely to have a meaningful understanding of the underlying ideas. Defining one word you do not understand with some collection of other words you do not understand does not constitute understanding, at least as I understand it.

Worse, it had been implicitly suggested to the students that the science lies in the terminology itself and that the only access to the science is through authority (teacher, textbook, Wikipedia…). Ignored is that to most students the authoritarian claim that "an object in motion tends to stay in motion with the same speed" is in stark contrast with what we see in the real world. Everything that we touch, drive, kick, or push comes to a stop if we watch it long enough. This was confounding to some of the greatest minds in history.

In class, there was no opportunity to observe (or even consider) multiple experiments in varying conditions that can lead a student to interpret what would happen to an object if left unaffected. There was no opportunity for them to see how they can assign a name to what they themselves can observe and reason through. This alone can be an extended lesson.

So can similar activities on force, net force, equilibrium, normal force, and other related terms.

As for the weight and gravity part of the lesson, I reviewed what was presented many times and I struggle with seeing what can be learned from it. Even after understanding force, acceleration, and Newton's second law, I am not sure what intellectual value there is in knowing the mathematical relationship among weight, mass, and the acceleration due to gravity (g), if there is no independent understanding of each of the three terms. One could plug in numbers for two of them to get the third, but so what? Where did it come from? What does it mean? When does it apply? Using one technical word to define another, either through text or equations, is fleeting and contrary to developing an operational understanding of the content or process of science.

Scientific ideas, concepts, and relationships were presented devoid of any scientific thought.

Finally, I agree with Mr. Lowrey about the value of asking students to complete the Regents exam early in the year, but I am concerned. While it might help test performance, it promotes a view of science as a collection of unmotivated, unsubstantiated pieces of information to be accepted, memorized, and repeated. When I teach more advanced material in college, I find this view of science to be a greater impediment to success than any missing piece of content knowledge or math skill. When I engage in dialogue outside of science, outside of the classroom, I find this approach a downright nuisance.

REFLECTIONS ON EPISTEMOLOGY, LAKEETA. TOMMY, AND MR. LOWREY

One definition of epistemology is "a branch of philosophy that investigates the origin, nature, methods, and limits of human knowledge." The difficulties that I saw from Lakeeta, Tommy, and so many others are epistemological. Their difficulties were more because of how they approached learning than weaknesses with math, language, or content knowledge. Teaching strategies used by teachers such as Mr. Lowrey, while evaluated as being successful, promote student approaches to learning which are contrary to science, reason, and inquiry. Results are contrary to preparation for success in college and beyond. A year at UHS showed me that they are also more ingrained than any misconception (or ignorance) about the content.

Meaningful educational strategies must promote effective epistemological approaches. This is important if we want our students to learn the content which we are trying to get them to understand. More importantly, it is critical if we want our students to think and learn more effectively in general. And even if there is a single-minded goal of success on a traditional standardized test, then it needs be recognized that effective epistemological approaches, strong thinking skills, and sound knowledge of the content go hand in hand (in hand).

STRATEGIES THAT WORK: EPISTEMOLOGY

There are instructional strategies that promote effective epistemological approaches, that get students to think about what they are doing. Students can estimate, explain their reasoning, justify how they know what is known, relate equations to concepts, connect classroom learning to the real world, and so on. These strategies might be uncomfortable and unfamiliar to many students, but they do meet with success. This success can grow when implemented systematically. My progress with Lakeeta, Tommy and their classmates might have been limited but it was real. Lack of greater progress was unfortunately a product of the sum total of their schooling and their expectations as to what school is.

Below I describe two relatively simple interactive activities related to the content covered by Mr. Lowrey. One is an interactive demonstration that focuses on Newton's First Law and inertia. The other is a kinesthetic laboratory activity that focuses on Newton's second law. These activities can be implemented in lab groups or as a whole class. Each exemplifies instruction which promotes effective epistemological approaches. Students make observations, describe them in their own words, and participate actively in making sense of important scientific concepts. In neither example are technical terms, formulae, or edict used to replace development of ideas. I have implemented each dozens of times. It is typically successful as gauged by students' affective response, students' understanding of the science content, and explicit student comments about how one comes to know science.

An interactive demonstration on Newton's First Law

I push a block on a table and then let go. The block slides and then comes to rest. "What did you observe?" I hear about friction, momentum, and lots of other things. We talk about the difference between an observation and an inference. We talk about describing the observation in simple terms that everyone can understand. I redirect the discussion to very simply what did you actually see the block do after it left my hand. They get to the point that they say they saw the block move in a particular direction, slow down, and stop.

Then I take out a block with the same size, shape, and appearance, except the bottom is unambiguously smoother. As best as I can, I give the second block the same initial push. "What did you observe?" This time I get observations. "The block moved, slowed down, and stopped." I ask for more. "It's purple." Good, but not quite where I was going. "It went farther." Okay. "It was slower." Wait, what does that mean? I gave them both similar initial pushes. They started with the same speed and then each slowed to a stop. "So what do you mean by slower?" "The second one took longer to slow down and stop." Now that is describing what just happened.

I ask someone up front to feel the bottom of each block. The first one is rougher. "What's up with that?" "Friction!" They know by now that's not what I am looking to hear. They eventually share with me other observations involving rough and smooth things. "When you rub rough things together they get hot." "It is harder for me to drag something across something that is rough than something that is smooth." Interesting. Students recognize that the roughness is doing something when there is rubbing. We call that something friction.

I don't have any more blocks, but I ask the students to predict what would happen if I had a third block with the same size, shape, and appearance, except the bottom is even smoother than the previous one. "It will take even longer to slow down and stop." Suppose I had a fourth block that was even smoother. What would happen then? What is the difference with all of these blocks? "The friction (now I let them use the word) must be making it so that the rougher blocks are slowing down. Less friction, less slowing down." What if there was no friction at all?

I take out a hover disc (or a low friction cart, or a block of dry ice). I give it a push on a large horizontal surface. Students watch what happens. They describe it in their own words.

Now we talk about bodies in motion staying in constant motion. Now we talk about inertia, and not by just repeating a bunch of words copied from the Internet.

A kinesthetic laboratory activity on Newton's Second Law

I roll a bowling ball across the floor. Clearly here is a body in motion staying in constant motion, at least until it hits something. Apparently friction is not playing a big role here.[5] Well, what if I didn't want it to stay in constant motion? "Kick it." "Push it." "Hit it with a mallet." Funny that should come up. I happen to have a mallet handy.

---

[5] Occasionally a student will say something about friction and bowling or about that the ball is rolling, but that does not usually come up nor does it matter much for this activity.

CHAPTER 3

Students in the class enter into a contest.[6] I place two cones on opposite sides of the room with nothing but empty floor in between. The contest is to take the bowling ball from rest at one cone to the other cone and back to the first cone, but there are rules. If these rules are broken, the result is disqualification. You can only hit the ball with the mallet. You can not push, guide or catch it. You can not go past either cone. The one with the smallest time without a disqualification wins.

The first student rushes from cone 1 to cone 2, then right at cone 2 gives a smack in the opposite direction only to find that the ball keeps flying past cone 1 anyway. "DQ." The second student repeats the same process, with a harder smack at cone 2. Same result, but not quite as pronounced. Regardless, the class is all over identifying the disqualification. The third student is intent to not have the ball pass the cone and goes at a snail's pace. I put the stopwatch down and sarcastically take out a calendar. Nevertheless, we have our first official time. Next student goes faster, but determined to not pass the cone ends up pushing the ball at cone 2 instead of hitting it. Subtle maybe, but still a DQ.

It usually takes six or seven contestants for someone to figure out how to get a competitive time without a DQ. Hit it aggressively several times forward and then just as aggressively and just as many times backwards. That means you have to start slowing the ball down well before cone 2. Does the ball always go the direction that the ball is hit? Clearly no. Can the ball move even when not being hit? Yep. So then what does the hit do? "Speeds it up." "Slows it down." "Changes the speed." For each segment of the motion, we identify which way the ball is hit, which way the ball is going, and which way the motion of the ball is changing. The hit and the way the motion is changing is always the same, but the velocity is not. A coincidence? I think not. Depending on the context, we might talk about force and acceleration.

What would happen if the mass were different? What would happen if you hit the ball with the mallet harder or softer? What would happen if there were more than one mallet hitting the ball?

Now we can talk about Newton's second law. I might be the one guiding the activities, but the students are the ones building their own understanding of the ideas.

GALILEO GALILEI

It is hard to dispute Galileo's brilliance as a scientist. I find his perspectives on the learning and understanding of science just as impressive. Judging from the first quote at the beginning of this chapter, I suspect that he would be just as concerned at the implications of the stories in this chapter as I am. Judging from the second quote, he would be just as excited about alternative strategies.

---

[6] I learned this (and so much more) when I was at the University of Maryland under the wonderful tutelage of Joe Redish. Dick Berg showed me fun things to do with a bowling ball that he learned from Joe and his colleagues Ed Taylor and Charles Misner.

F$#%ING BALL

Classroom management

Bodily exercise, when compulsory, does no harm to the body; but knowledge which is acquired under compulsion obtains no hold on the mind.

- Plato

OCTOBER 9: WHAT DID SHE SAY?

No conversation about being a first year teacher would be complete without including classroom management. It is what new teachers ask for help with most. It is the main reason that New York City teachers leave teaching altogether.

I have always been comfortable and friendly around kids of all ages. I know the subject matter and the most contemporary classroom strategies, both in physics and in general. I have a well developed model of how students learn. I speak comfortably about topics of interest to teenagers, with a reasonably thick New York accent to boot. Therefore, despite the dire warnings, I started at UHS confident that I would be able to handle classroom management. I was wrong.

Most first year teachers (or second, or third…) can write a book filled with examples of students talking in class, walking in late, not doing work, misusing classroom materials, falling asleep, copying homework, or using the most recent electronic gizmo when they should be working. I experienced all of this. The disruption to my teaching was significant. Most first year teachers (or second, or third…) in New York City have had students curse at them, threaten them (implicitly or explicitly), violate their personal property, and fabricate claims of misconduct about them. I experienced all of that too. The disruption to my psyche was significant. Without a doubt, classroom management, however defined, was the most stressful and prominent feature of my teaching at UHS.

In order to paint a complete picture of my sabbatical, I describe experiences related to classroom management. In order to maintain focus, I describe experiences which were most directly related to me trying to teach by inquiry.

For example, there was the week in early October that I did the mallet and bowling bowl activity described at the end of last chapter. After all of the challenges getting students engaged, excited, learning, and off of their cell phones, I was excited to implement my sure fire happy learning game. True to form, many of the students bought in. Whether they liked it or not, they got a kinesthetic foundation of inertia, force, and Newton's second law. They were also engaged in and excited about the activity.

Of the three classes in which I did the bowling ball contest, Period 1 was the one that I was looking forward to most. Every day this was the class that gave me the most problems. At least this one day I thought I would have success. That was until it was Melisha's turn.

Melisha was not a good student. Her attendance was sporadic. Her math, literacy, and reasoning skills were well below grade level. When she showed up to class, she did not do her work. She was never afraid to say what she was thinking about any topic at any time, but physics never seemed to come up. I found her disrespectful. Her other teachers had similar opinions about her.

Surprisingly, Melisha was one of the first to volunteer to try the bowling ball challenge. She gave it a good effort. Like most students though, she did not plan it right and the bowling ball went flying past the cone into a lab stool. I was thinking what a great learning opportunity. Melisha didn't see it that way. She threw the mallet across the room, kicked over the stool, and shouted "F$#%ing ball." Unapologetic, she continued to rant, regardless of what I had to say.

I was 10 minutes into a double period with my best lesson and there I was exhorting the class to not laugh, get back in their seats, and do some busy work while I was seeking help from the Dean. The lesson and opportunity for redirection with a difficult class were shot.

BUMMER

Throughout my sabbatical, I kept a journal. I wrote about logistics, quotes, stories, reflections, classroom activities, and so on. I also wrote about my thoughts and feelings. Two entries in my journal from October were:

I like teaching and the kids a lot, but it is getting less fun. I prefer the disposition that I usually have (humorous, friendly, open to dialogue, encouraging of questions and group work, not getting kids in trouble) but when I am meaner and more rigid it is easier on me. Also, they learn more when they are actually doing something but behave better when I am writing lots of stuff on the board for them to copy down.

There is a significant minority of students who are intent on disrupting class. They are disrespectful, rude, loud, and persistently in need of my attention during class time. I think that I am handling it okay, but at a cost I do not like. I spend too much of my time and energy focusing on control. My approaches and thoughts are on these students instead of what I believe to be the majority who would do very well with the usual me.

There has got to be a better way. I was determined to work it out.

TWO TEACHERS WHO DID NOT HAVE PROBLEMS WITH CLASSROOM MANAGEMENT (AND NEITHER OF THEM WERE ME)

My nightmare of difficulties under the umbrella of classroom management was frustrating. My faith that I could figure it out though remained strong as I visited so many other teachers who did not have the problems that I had. Most of them had much more classroom experience than me.

For example, there was Ms. O'Brien. She was an older, soft spoken, history teacher. When I visited her class, everyone showed up on time with their homework done. They were in their assigned seats with their books open. Ms. O'Brien led a discussion about the life and times of colonial America. Students examined original works. They actively debated perspectives of members of different communities of the time. Most of the students eagerly and respectfully raised their hands to contribute constructively. Conversation continued beyond the time Ms. O'Brien had allotted. She had to cut off enthusiastic participants as the class period neared the end.

Ms. Williams, another experienced teacher, also had no problems with classroom management. She was nothing like Ms. O'Brien though, in class or out. She was clearly not happy about being a teacher and seemed jaded. The day that I visited her class she assigned a math worksheet. From my vantage in the back of the room it looked like busy work. Students were visibly disinterested, but none of them were acting out. As I watched for a while it became clear why. Ms. Williams shouted at students for as little as looking away from their worksheets. (Even I was afraid that she would come over to my desk to see what I was doing.) She used intimidation, threats, and punishment to demand the behavior that she wanted, and she got it.

Neither Ms. O'Brien nor Ms. Williams had the difficulty with classroom management that I had, but for different reasons. I saw respected successful teachers like Ms. O'Brien have no problems with classroom management. However I also saw equally skilled and motivated teachers fail with similar techniques. I saw intimidating teachers like Ms. Williams use control and authority to successfully manage classrooms. However I also saw equally loud and threatening teachers end up with some of the most unruly classes. It did not appear obvious to me whether either strategy by itself dictates good classroom management.

There were other teachers who used more subtle control methods as a primary management technique. For example, I saw many teachers use comprehensive point accumulation plans resulting in extra credit, lower grades, or calls home. These also resulted in mixed success.

I also did not always see a correlation between classroom management and the extent to which inquiry-based activities were implemented. Ms. O'Brien and Ms. Williams were on the opposite ends of the inquiry approach. Each had a control of the class, albeit a very different kind of control. All other combinations of inquiry instruction and classroom management existed.

I will save for separate chapters how making meaningful connections with students and their lives seemed a common feature to those who had the most deep-seated success. Connecting with students the right way led to integrating good classroom management with good teaching.

PLANETS BY INQUIRY?

Too often I observed instruction with weak epistemological approaches like those described in the last chapter. Fortunately (unfortunately?), with the right (wrong?) instructor, these were accompanied with obedience and fewer behavioral disruptions. Students chanted, recited, read, and parroted. These are all tasks low on Bloom's taxonomy of learning objectives.[1] Apparently tasks without much thinking involved can lead to a kind of classroom order valued by many teachers and administrators.

As an example, students worked on the worksheet shown in Figure 4.1.[2] These represent the kind of questions that can be answered without much thinking, activity, resistance, or trouble, other than a possible digression about whether Pluto is a planet.

Vocabulary:
_____ : natural or artificial object orbiting in space.

Check: Match each planet with its correct moon.
1.	Jupiter	a.	Charon
2.	Mars	b.	Triton
3.	Uranus	c.	Io
4.	Pluto	d.	Titania
5.	Neptune	e.	Titan
6.	Saturn	f.	Phobos

Apply: Answer the following. Please use complete sentences.
Which planet moves faster in its orbit, Mercury or Pluto?

_____
_____

Figure 4.1. Traditional worksheet implemented in earth science class about planets.

In contrast to the worksheet, when I taught about planets I asked the students to be active physically and cognitively. They made observations of the different planets via a computer simulation. Then they described specifically how they can account for the motion of the planets in each the geocentric and heliocentric models of the solar system. They had to get up, move around, consider different

---

[1] On the low end of the oft-cited Bloom's taxonomy are activities like recalling, repeating, and naming. On the high end are activities like analyzing, formulating, and evaluating.

[2] I found this handout in the copy room. I do not know who used it or how it went, but I have a pretty good guess.

models and visual perspectives, and negotiate answers with each other. These activities left me much more vulnerable to disruption and dissention. (Some students seized on this vulnerability, most did the opposite.) I did them anyway. I'll do them again next time too.

GARRY, MARLON, AND ROBINSON

Although still challenging, my period 7 class was always my easiest. The behavioral reputations and academic success rates of the students in this section were similar to my other sections. The curriculum, class size, and physical space were all about the same. I don't know why, but the class dynamic was always good for this class and it just went better. By all accounts, this was the class where there was the least problem with classroom management.

Garry's name had been on my period 7 roster from the beginning of the year, but he did not show up to a single class the first two months. Then one day, halfway through period 7, in walked someone I had never seen. "Can I help you?" "I'm Garry." He starts chatting with the person next to him. "Please sit over here." (School rules require assigned seats.) No response. "Please sit over here." "I don't like teachers with an attitude, because then I get an attitude."

The class, usually upbeat and participatory, sat quiet. After some refusing, cursing, and a racial remark by Garry, I wrote him up and sent him to the "resource room" not ten minutes after meeting him for the first time.

It went downhill from there. Very little time and inquiries revealed to me that Garry had a long history of disruptive and even criminal behavior in school. Garry was not and apparently never had any intention of taking school seriously. Yet there he was, 17 years old, right back in the classroom. I suffered as he single-handedly transformed a relatively productive class through his presence and shift of my focus. The class suffered too. There were not a lot of Garrys, but they caused a lot of problems.

Marlon was in my period 1 class. He was a bright young man who had no intentions of passing physics despite being perfectly capable of doing well. His grades in other classes were all over the place. He had a reputation of getting into trouble, but not big trouble.

Marlon did not do class work, usually did not turn in homework, and would find any reason (other than science) to argue with me. When it came time to predict which object would hit the target first in a classroom demonstration, Marlon sat quiet. When it came time to remind the class of school policy about bathroom passes Marlon would spend ten minutes debating it with me. When Marlon was at the line where I would write him up or call his home, he backed down, but never sooner. Each day he sought that line with me.

Robinson was a strong student. He was also mature and popular with his classmates. When I worked with him on any academic material he showed great aptitude and interest. He was intellectually similar to the students who I worked with every summer in the Summer Scholars Program. He was a pleasure to talk to about school work and anything else.

Robinson never got into trouble in my class, although one comment might have upset another teacher. With my focus firmly on the Garrys and the Marlons of the school, one day I went over a simple problem ad nauseam. I told the class that they needed to know it for the next test. I asked everyone if they had any question that they should ask right then. There were no questions. I then asked them to clear their desks for a surprise quiz.

The quiz was the exact question that I had just gone over. Many had no idea how to do it, but this was a trivial problem for Robinson. Regardless, with an uncharacteristically nasty tone, he said "This is crazy. We're not learning nothing." I was furious. Not at Robinson, but at myself. (I later apologized to Robinson.) Why was it that Robinson did not drive curriculum and instruction? Why was this bright, motivated, young man not the focus of my attention?

Despite his behavior, Garry stayed in my class. He knew the system better than I did. He knew that he would remain in the school, by and large on his terms. On the days that he showed up, he single-handedly transformed what was a productive me and productive class into a rigid, discipline-focused forty-two minutes of misery.

Marlon never wanted to get into real trouble. He was accurate in recognizing he was nowhere near real trouble or unacceptable consequences, at least unacceptable to him. After all, he knew Garry well. School and his friends and his entertainment were Marlon's entitlement and if he wanted to harass me, so be it. If there was a low grade or a referral in his file, not a problem, tomorrow was another day.

Robinson was the one who suffered because of the presence of all the Marlons and Garrys. There were a lot of Robinsons.

THE RULES NEED TO CHANGE

The support system (in *and* out of school) should have been set up so that Garry was not such an angry self-destructive young man. It wasn't. Garry had become a disruptive high school student impervious to redirection.

In my opinion, a student removal process was needed for Garry.[3] Such a process would have re-established my period 7 class (and likely Garry's other classes) as successful. Inquiry learning with experimental materials would have again been possible. Such a process would have changed the expectations of Marlon, who wanted to be in school and out of trouble, but existed in a culture where he was encouraged to behave the way he did. Most of all it would have helped all the Robinsons, who were victims of redistributed school resources, time, and focus.

My request for Garry's removal based on numerous incidents with multiple teachers was denied. Although never stated to me outright, apparently not only is removing a student from school an incredibly high hurdle, it is also a negative score for the school in the school assessment system.

---

[3] A similar process for Melisha would have been inevitable, but she left the school for unrelated reasons soon after the bowling ball incident.

A STICKY SOLUTION

I thought that the bowling ball activity would be a hit (no pun intended). I thought the time that I took them outside to throw a ball up and figure out how fast it was launched would be even better. Those two were mixed bags. For whatever reason though, they loved the transparent tape activity similar to the one described at the end of chapter 2. Even Marlon was pulling up the tape and going over to the next table to see if the same thing was happening there. Almost everyone had something to say about what they were seeing and what could be causing it. Follow up class discussion about the nature of charge went just as well and was just as on task. Score one for inquiry learning helping with classroom management.

REFLECTIONS ON INQUIRY SCIENCE, CLASSROOM MANAGEMENT, AND RESPONSIBILITY

I know that I barely touched on the myriad of complex, interacting issues related to Marlon, Garry, Robinson, Ms. O'Brien, Ms. Williams, and classroom management. However, these observations and perspectives were an important part of my trying to be a successful science teacher at UHS.

As is typically the case, in many teacher education classes at CCNY we teach that if you get the students doing something that is interesting, educational, and meaningful, there will be far fewer problems with classroom management. I still believe this is true... to an extent. The instructional strategies and approaches described throughout this book need be part of the solution, but there needs to be an institutional commitment to it at all levels. I saw how successful classroom management can go hand in hand with successful instruction with Ms. O'Brien (and many others) and with the transparent tape lab (and many others). The problem was that these were the exceptions, both from the perspective of the school and from the perspective of the student. What would happen if these were the norm? I argue that the answer is much better overall classroom management in any school setting.

And I can't help but wonder what would happen if on top of good instruction the students saw school as a privilege and not an entitlement, a feat more likely if it were more meaningful, student-centered, and effective. Garry needed to be removed from the school. Marlon needed to adjust or leave as well. (He would have adjusted.) High school as they made it was a waste of their time, my time, and lots of money. Force feeding education changed nothing for them, but it resulted in Robinson suffering. Students with less academic skill than Robinson but who wanted an education also suffered. And nothing was gained by Garry staying.

STRATEGIES THAT WORK: CLASSROOM MANAGEMENT

As described above, I often saw good inquiry-based instruction correlate with fewer classroom management problems, even if the correlation was not as high as I would have liked. Below are two classroom activities which I have had simultaneous success with student learning and with classroom management.

The first activity is group testing. Groups of three to four each get a different question and are told to submit a single group solution for a grade. In all my years of teaching at all levels to all audiences, never is there more productive and directed learning then when students work on a test question together. Never is there less need for me to intervene about any classroom dynamic. I recognize that there can be discomfort among some students and teachers when there is a group test question. Regardless, this is a strategy I have tried with wonderful results and I believe there is carryover to non-test class activities. I take great care in grouping students and selecting appropriate questions. I mitigate concerns about fairness by making the group test only a small fraction of the total test score. I also inform the students that I am simultaneously grading the entire group on the extent to which I see them work collaboratively. Never have I seen a group struggle to do so on a group test.

The group test question shown below is on calorimetry. It is at the advanced high school / lower division college level. One of the things that makes this question work well as a group question is that it is usually too hard for a single student to solve quickly. Almost all students initially set up the problem mathematically without accounting for the phase change or the presence of three materials all changing temperature, resulting in the wrong answer. The wrong approach usually gives rise to a solution where liquid water is over 100°C, which is not possible physically. Often one student will attempt the problem naively, a second student will recognize the flaw in the strategy, and the group will collaborate on a multi-step problem solving strategy. Since there are multiple distinct paths to a solution, this conversation can be very rich and include strategies for checking the group's solution.

The second activity is simulations of scientific phenomena. It should not be surprising that today's students feel comfortable in a virtual reality, changing the rules of some computer play world and then exploring what happens. What a great opportunity to leverage this familiarity to learn science! Students could see how changing external conditions affects molecular motion or how changing circuit parameters influences electron behavior. They could control the environment of mythical creatures and see how evolution unfolds after many generations or they could breed animals with different features to see what their offspring would look like. Along the way, even the most challenging students can stay productively engaged.

The "electric field hockey" simulation described below is a program from the PhET project developed at the University of Colorado.[4] In this simulation, students place charges at different locations with the objective of projecting a target charge through an obstacle and into a goal. It looks and feels like a video game, except that the underlying principals are driven by fundamental physics. In playing the game, a student can't help but to learn about electrical interactions and the relationship between force and motion, even if by accident.

---

[4] This simulation, and many others, is available at http://phet.colorado.edu/. For sample research on student learning with simulations, see http://phet.colorado.edu/en/research.

Group test question on colorimetry

Include names of all group members on the submitted solution. A portion of your grade will be determined by the extent to which your entire group is working collaboratively.[5]

A 0.75 kg piece of aluminum is initially at a temperature of 550°C. The aluminum is transferred to a 1.00 kg insulated iron container with 1.00 kg of water. Both the iron and the water are at 85.0°C. Determine the final equilibrium state and temperature of the entire system. Show all work and explain your reasoning.

Electric field hockey simulation

Launch the program "Electric field hockey."

1. For each of the levels arrange the blue and red charges so that the black charge is launched into the goal without colliding with an obstacle. Repeat this process using the minimum number of blue and red charges possible. Sketch at least one arrangement of charges that results in a goal.

2. What is the relationship between the electric field vector direction and the force vector direction? Explain how you can tell using the features of the program.

3. Is the direction of the motion always in the direction of the force? Explain how your answer is consistent with Newton's laws.

PLATO

Even though Plato's words about the limits of forced learning are some 2500 years old, they still ring true. Every one of my experiences as a teacher, parent, and researcher supports the contemporary findings of cognitive scientists, educational psychologists, neurobiologists, science education researchers, and my mother that telling someone to know something is not an effective way to get them to learn. Yet there are so many classes, teachers, textbooks, Internet sites, and lab directions telling the students what to do and think. Kids do not learn well this way. Anything they "learn" is fleeting. There is also a lost opportunity for constructive engagement to be the primary focus. There is a lost opportunity for students to *want* to do what you want them to do.

---

[5] Relevant physical constants are provided for the students, including ones (such as the latent heat of fusion of Al) that are not relevant for this problem.

THE AVERAGE OF 36 AND 38 IS 57

Math literacy

However beautiful the strategy, you should occasionally look at the results.

- Winston Churchill

NOVEMBER 18: APPLIED MATH?

Every week with my Regents physics classes, per state mandate, the students conducted a "science laboratory." I applaud the mandate. However I put science laboratory in quotes because so many of the labs that I saw implemented, published, and on line were procedures that I would not call science. I would also not call them laboratory activities. I certainly would not call them educational.

As Thanksgiving approached, I had the students conduct a standard lab on the pendulum. They did the usual thing about measuring the period for different values of mass and string length. They graphed their results. The steps were laid out clearly for the students. They were told exactly what to vary, how many times to vary it, what to write down, what to graph, and what to calculate. I was bored just reading it, but this particular week I chose the path of least resistance and used it anyway.

At one point, students were told to graph the period squared vs. length of the pendulum. As was often the case, I saw students unable to implement math skills that they should have mastered well before taking physics in eleventh grade. Students in my classes certainly did not have mastery of graphing. From setting up the scales to plotting the numbers, students struggled. Understanding why they were doing what they were doing was not up for discussion. Interpreting the slope of any line was way too ambitious. My hope of contrasting why one draws a smooth curve through the data instead of playing connect the dots never even came up, and that was probably the most important lesson that could have occurred that day.[1]

Another lab required that students measure volume reading on a graduated cylinder. To improve accuracy, each group was asked to measure it twice and take the average. Taking the average of numbers was another math skill certainly expected of eleventh graders,

---

[1] When data is taken, the points do not lie along a smooth line or curve. Understanding experimental uncertainty and how to model data should have been an important lesson for this lab, more important than anything that they were learning about the pendulum.

Table 4 in my period 7 class had four of my stronger students. These four young women understood the material well and routinely worked well in class. Unlike most of the tables, I could always count on them to do a good job, even when I was not standing over them.

The four students were dutifully working together on the lab when I went to their station to see how they were doing. As usual, they were on task and going through the handout. They had done two independent measurements of the same volume and had calculated the average. The two measurements were 36 ml and 38 ml. The average that they calculated was 57 ml.

Me: *You got that the average of 36 and 38 is 57?*

Lisaura: *Yes.*

Me: *Does that make sense?*

Lisa: *Yes.*

Me: *Are you sure?*

(Multiple students fumble with their calculators.)

Sanaya: *Wait a second. It's 37.*

Eleventh grade students should be able to calculate averages easily and reliably. These good students could not. Eleventh grade students should recognize that there was no way that 57 could be the average of 36 and 38. Nope. Eleventh grade students should have recognized that it made no sense to write down 57 ml as a reasonable volume for what they had just measured. (The reading on the cylinder was clearly in the thirties.) This did not even occur to my model group.

Student difficulties with math were of course not limited to lab. For example, my Do Now was often a math question. I tried to make it a question related to the math that they needed to apply that day, but in a way that it looked more familiar.

When covering vector components, one of my Do Now's was to find the length of the legs of a right triangle. Students needed help with the trigonometry even before I got to the vectors. They then needed help recognizing that finding vector components was the same thing as finding the legs of a right triangle despite the superficial differences in the appearance of the two situations. Finding the legs of a right triangle was something they had all seen in their math classes for years.

When covering motion in one dimension, one of my Do Now's was to solve $5x = 80$. Unfortunately, too many students wrote $x = 75$. Students did not see $5x = 80$ as an equation where you are trying to find out what multiplied by 5 is 80 or how many 5's go into 80. These kinds of viewpoints are critical in so many ways in applying math to science. It needs to be automatic and clear. Instead, students tried to remember the procedure that they were told to use to solve an equation that looks like this, a much less useful approach.

Worse, they did not even remember the procedure. "Do I divide both sides by 5 or do I subtract 5 from both sides?" If there is no understanding of why the procedure is the way it is, I am not sure how valuable it is to remember it. Students did not understand why. Students did not remember the procedure. I do not see this as a coincidence.

Students consistently struggled with math skills that were supposed to have been mastered in earlier grades. Algebra, trigonometry, graphs, averages, and even multiplication were constantly misunderstood and then misapplied. The problem was not just with their math skills. Their epistemological approaches interfered with their chance to succeed in learning and applying math. Failure to memorize a procedure is problematic. Believing that memorizing a procedure is learning math is disastrous.

Ironically, the math skills with which I saw students struggle were the very ones that I saw drilled into students in math classes that I visited. The mandate was that students know this stuff and be tested precisely on it. Teachers tried relentlessly to get students to know the skills by teaching it directly, often forcefully. Kids just had to be ready by test day. Based on what I saw in my physics classes, this strategy was not a good one for the long term.

HELP!

Reviewing my journal after my sabbatical was over, I was amused by the following entry:

Help, I've fallen and I can't get up. I am sick, behind on my grading, trying to plan curriculum, and have not made progress with so many students. I am tired, worn down and holiday break is still a month away.

Wow, being a teacher is hard!

COULOMB'S LAW OR COULOMB'S LAWS?

Coulomb's law is the mathematical relationship that describes the force between charges. The force is a constant (k) times the product of the magnitude of the two charges (q_1 and q_2) divided by the square of the distance between the two charges (r). It is written something like:

$$F = k \frac{q_1 q_2}{r^2}$$

This might look somewhat intimidating to high school students, but the math is just multiplication and division. I did not think that my students were coming in with an understanding of Coulomb's law. However, I thought that they were coming in with enough mastery in math that they could plug numbers into this equation to calculate force.

After a few days working on Coulomb's laws, some of the more attentive students were agitated. In working through a sample problem, I wrote on the board:

$$F = \frac{kq_1q_2}{r^2}$$

"What is that?" "That's not right!" Never mind *their* confusion, *I* was the one baffled. We had worked with this equation for multiple examples. Why so up in arms now?

I let them go on: "That's not the equation that we have been using. Why did you change it?" It took me a few minutes to realize what they were saying. The difference the students were referring to was the location of the *k*. I saw the two versions of Coulomb's law as identical and expected the students to have seen it as the same. They did not.

Multiplication, fractions, and even the associative property were all math skills that should have been mastered well before eleventh grade. They were not. The difference in the location of that *k* does not change the equation. I think that if there were numbers instead of symbols in the equation that after a while students would have been able to use their calculators to recognize that the two equations were the same. But this is not good enough. A reasonable conceptual understanding of the basic properties of multiplication should have students seeing the two relationships above as identical right away.

MOTION SENSORS

One of the lessons that went particularly well was the motion sensor lab. Motion sensors are small devices hooked up to a computer that use sonar to measure the location of an object. I had the students walk towards and away from the sensor. The computer plotted graphs of their motion right in front of students as they walked.

Students explored questions like: What happens when you walk towards the sensor? away from it? What happens when you speed up? slow down? How does the position graph relate to the velocity graph? Can you walk in a way that creates a particular shaped graph? Can you predict what position and velocity graphs will look like if you walk in a way that someone else describes?

At least on that day, my students developed some conceptual foundation of position, velocity, and acceleration. Coming into the activity, my students did not have an understanding of the tools of high school math that I wanted. Here was an activity where they improved their understanding of graphical representations and slope. Having students apply the tools in a meaningful context improved their understanding of those tools and their application.

The funny thing is that if I had just tried to drill the graphing skills into my students, like I saw happen in so many math classes, I don't think they would have learned them nearly as well. If I had tried to tell them the difference between velocity and acceleration with just formulas and jargon, I don't think they would have learned those concepts nearly as well. And if I had focused my instruction on material which looked just like what would be on the Regents, I don't think I would have even worked with motion sensors.

NO WAY!

Monica was working on a physics problem. She got to the point where the solution was seventy-four times one. She took out her calculator and pushed "seventy-four times one equals" to get the answer.[2]

This was not be the only time I saw a student use a calculator to multiply a number by one.

RATIO ABUSE

There were many times where students had to set up ratios to solve for something that they were looking for. If given the mass of some volume of a substance, what is the mass of a different volume of the same substance? If given the distance a ball travels in some time interval at a constant speed, how far does it travel in a different time interval? If given the size of a shadow of an object some distance from a screen, how big would the shadow be for a different distance?

Students always started problems like these with something like "This is to that as this is to that." Often they were right in setting up the proper ratio. Depending on the particulars, they often solved for the unknown correctly. However they never quite convinced me that they knew what they were doing.

We were solving a distance along a curve problem and I wanted to pursue students' real understanding. The way it is usually presented, the ratio of an arc length to the interior angle given is equal to ratio of the circumference to 360°.

Many set up the ratio for the problem that we were working correctly and stated "This is to that as this is to that. It's a ratio!" I wanted to know how it was that they knew that specific equation would yield the correct result. The explanations were never more than a restatement of it being a ratio and that's how math works. Never did I hear about how many of those particular interior angles were in the entire 360° of the circle. Never did I hear about the relationship between the interior angle and the arc length or the arc length and the circumference. Worse, I never saw students recognize their lack of understanding of where it was that the equation came from.

It was almost as though there was an unspoken contract between teacher and student. The teacher made sure to ask the question in such a way that the student would get the correct answer by using the "this is to that" technique. All teachers

---

[2]   74

knew what strategy they were going to use. We all knew if we just asked the question the right way that they would get the right answer. The student then agreed to follow through with a correct answer and not ask questions about why to do it that way. Quid pro quo.

Of course this did not work for me. I tweaked the delivery of one of the examples. I changed it so that the given was not the very interior angle that would make the setting of the equality of ratios so easy to get correct by accident. Sure enough, everyone struggled. They just hooked up the small angle given with the small length given and proceeded to the "This is to that as this is to that" strategy. Never mind that the approach was faulty and the answer was off by a factor of 10.

There it was. I decided to break the contract. I was hoping that this would inspire a desire in the students to know how to apply math techniques to solve real world science problems meaningfully. Instead it generated frustration and rebellion. I was accused of just trying to "trick" them.

For the rest of the year I waffled. Do I challenge student mathematical insight? Or do I make sure to present the problem so that even if they had no idea what they were doing they would have a chance to get the correct answer anyway? Unfortunately the latter approach was easier and far less stressful to execute.

OF BASIC MATH AND TAU NEUTRINOS

On a quiz, I included the following old physics Regents question:

> *The tau neutrino, the muon neutrino, and the electron neutrino are all:*

> *(1) leptons   (2) hadrons   (3) baryons   (4) mesons*

82% of the students answered this question correctly.[3] I could not help but juxtapose this result with these same students struggling to average 2 numbers, make a graph, or know how fast a car is going when they are told how fast the car is going. As far as I am concerned, my students did not have the chance to know the difference between a neutrino and Newfoundland. The 82% "success rate" is a gross misrepresentation of my students' understanding of anything.

I did not see any value in imposing that students in my school understand neutrinos, decay modes of radioactive isotopes, or eccentricity of the planets' elliptical motion.[4] Covering these topics in high school science does harm to the future of scientific literacy in this country. It lowers academic standards. It was clear to me that my students were not able to apply or understand topics like this. It was clear that they would not long remember these pieces of information. They also did not care. I did not see a single exception in any of my classes at UHS.

It was even worse than that. With the way that these topics were taught, students were developing a perverted understanding of what science is and how scientific

---

[3]   As I am writing this, I do not know the correct answer to this question. I would need to look it up on the reference table.

[4]   These are Regents topics in Physics, Chemistry, and Earth Science respectively.

ideas come to be known. There was a lost opportunity to have students work towards a real level of scientific literacy. There was also a lost opportunity to have students learn math skills more effectively in context. Ironically (tragically?), if students participated in real science learning over fewer topics, they would have come away understanding a greater breadth of science content and greater expertise with math skills in context.

REFLECTIONS ON STUDENT LEARNING OF MATH

My students at UHS had been through more than ten grades of math lessons and standardized tests. They had taken multiple Regents math classes. When they got to my class, they were unable to demonstrate understanding of what they had covered all those years or apply the skills reliably.

My observations suggest that the teaching of math to these kids was procedural, algorithmic, and not by inquiry. They were taught what steps to conduct to do the operations of whatever level they were in, de-contextualized from anything else in their lives except the big test at the end of the year. They left not knowing the procedures. They left not knowing the reasons that underlie those procedures. They did not have an epistemological approach to mathematical problem solving that facilitated them figuring out what makes sense or how to apply the math in unfamiliar settings.

The mathematical teaching of these kids failed. Although not discussed here, I suspect that a parallel story line could be presented for literacy skills as well. Students were not where they needed to be to take high school physics. They were certainly not near ready for real college work.

Everything I saw at UHS kept telling me that mandating or insisting that students be proficient with math does not work. Giving them the time and opportunity to build and apply needed skills in context does. Giving them the opportunity to develop an understanding of the underlying ideas as they go is critical.

Students must be proficient in math and literacy by the time they are deep into high school. Mine were not. I understand the call for tests that assure that skills are in place. I understand the call for students to succeed on these tests. This is not happening. Regardless of what you think of existing strategies, we need to look at the results.

STRATEGIES THAT WORK: MATHEMATICS

It was with a great feeling of satisfaction that I saw the motion sensor activity succeed with helping students learn mathematics in context, simultaneous to learning the science. This was not the only time. I often found that understanding of mathematics grew when students were engaged with the very science that I was trying to teach. Below are other examples.

The estimation problems serve many purposes in a science class, and I would even ask them to a class filled with students who have complete facility in the relevant mathematics. None of my classes were filled with students who had complete facility in the relevant mathematics. Therefore, these problems became wonderful opportunities to develop basic math skills couched in problems where math had to be done. In context, students worked on proportional reasoning, algebra, unit conversions, scientific notation, significant figures, and more. With my help, errors led to answers recognized as nonsensical and student directed attempts to diagnose the problems and correct them. Of course this was opportunity to refine and practice the math skills which were being exercised.

The second example shown below is a written exercise relating position, displacement, velocity, and acceleration to each other and to a velocity-time graph. I have found it to be a good follow up to the motion sensor activity with respect to learning the physics concepts and the associated math. To answer the questions, students need to interpret and contrast the meaning of the value of the graph and the meaning of the slope of the graph. They need to develop and apply a mathematical strategy to quantitatively determine the displacement of an object based on a graph of velocity. Since there are multiple ways to calculate the displacement, this leads to opportunities for group work and/or teaching students how to check their own answers. Finally, in the last part, students need to identify that there is not enough information to answer the question, regardless of any attempt to apply a formula which looks like it might be relevant.

Estimation problems

For the first 2 problems, a ruler, a ream of paper, and a physics text book are placed strategically within view of the class.

Estimate the thickness of a sheet of paper. Explain how you determined your answer.

Estimate how many physics textbooks can fit in the empire state building. Explain how you determined your answer.

Estimate how high a major league pitcher can throw a baseball straight up. Explain how you determined your answer.

Estimate the number of atoms in a copper penny. Explain how you determined your answer.

Motion graphing problem

Two cars travel in one dimension along side-by-side tracks with velocity vs. time graphs as shown below.

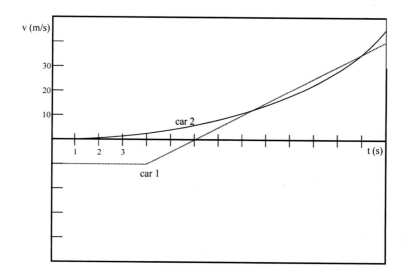

1. At what time(s), if any, is the velocity of car 1 equal to the velocity of car 2 at the same moment in time? Explain your reasoning.

2. At what time(s), if any, is the acceleration of car 1 equal to the acceleration of car 2 at the same moment in time? Explain your reasoning.

3. Find the displacement of car 1 between t=0 seconds and t=14 seconds. Explain how you determined your answer.

4. At what time(s), if any, is the position of car 1 equal to the position of car 2? Explain how you determined your answer.

WINSTON CHURCHILL

Winston Churchill was not thinking about education when he quipped about strategies and results, but his comment sure sounds relevant here. My students had been through a cycle of traditional instruction and assessment. They came to me without any reasonable baseline for success in applying, or even remembering, what they learned. Requiring students to cover material the way they are and then testing them the way we do is not working. I saw the results.

HOW AM I SUPPOSED TO KNOW WHAT TO DO IF YOU DON'T TELL ME?:

Independent learning

Whoever in discussion adduces authority uses not intellect but rather memory.

- Leonardo da Vinci

DECEMBER 6: TELL ME!

In early-December, I ran a lab on density. It was mostly traditional, but I thought this particular lab would work reasonably well and be educational. Students were given explicit instructions on how to measure volume (put water in graduated cylinder, measure the level of the water, put pennies in the water, ...). There was some confusion, such as students putting the entire graduated cylinder on the triple beam balance,[1] but eventually most were able to follow the steps.

Later in the lab, immediately after measuring the volume of two pennies, students were directed to measure the volume of four pennies. Hands went up. "How do I do that?" There was no spontaneous connection to the steps that they had just completed a few minutes earlier. They were shown explicitly how to measure the volume of two pennies. I guess that they were expecting to be shown explicitly the steps of how to measure the volume of four pennies (even though they were the same steps).

Students eventually measured volume and mass of two pennies, then four, and so on so that they could draw a graph and interpret its slope. Again I hoped to develop experimental technique, uncertainty, graphing, and best fit lines, but I never got to these real lessons of science in the lab.

Despite everything that I saw in earlier months, I was still surprised to see how poor the results were. Students wrote in their lab reports that more pennies resulted in less mass. They recorded that volume for multiple coins was "zero." What was most shocking though was that there was no recognition that these data must be flawed. Results were put on the graph, students connected the dots, and hands were again raised "What do I do now?" as if all was well.

In my journal I reflected that:

---

[1] I am not sure if they were trying to measure mass of the water without regard to the mass of the rather large graduated cylinder or if they were trying to determine the volume of the water with the triple beam balance.

Labs, and class work in general, are about students doing the steps that they are told to do without asking "Does that make sense?" or "How do I know that?" or "Can I connect what I am doing in my class to what I see in the world around me?"

The biggest obstacle to success is NOT limitations with math skills or knowing the definition of density or being able to read a triple beam balance. It is the institutional suppression of thinking.

Even the best students are trained to take an approach of wanting to be told what to do. They care about their grades. They recognize that most measures of success are based on traditional exams. This breeds an approach to learning by authority. I had this feeling all year. It seemed that every time I got strong students to encounter an interesting problem or a genuine learning opportunity, they just wanted the answer. In my journal I wrote:

The "good / smart" students do really try and care. However, they are entirely focused on an approach of "tell me what I have to do to get a good grade" and "just tell me what you want me to write / say" instead of focusing on "how can I learn and become smarter?"

This is valued implicitly, and sometimes explicitly, by the school system.

FIGURE IT OUT YOURSELF

Soon after the density lab, I was scheduled to do the related buoyancy lab. A fellow science teacher gave me one of those explicit step by step fill in the table type handouts to use. Students were told explicitly what to measure, tabulate, and calculate each step of the way. It really looked foolproof (no sarcasm intended) and like a logical follow up to the density lab.

Even though this lab would have been easy to set up and implement, I decided to write my own this time. Despite all of the challenges I was incurring (or maybe because of them) I was determined to try a lab more consistent with the scientific approaches that I believed in. These students had already gone through the related topics of measuring force, volume of water displaced, and how to calculate density in the density lab. They had studied these topics in class as well. I wanted to build on all of this in the buoyancy lab. I reasoned that by mid December they should be able to take more responsibility to find and understand the effect of buoyancy. I don't think that I went too far with the new lab. I just left things a little less directed.

Implementation did not go well. Students had no idea how to start or proceed. They would not think for more than 30 seconds (if at all) before complaining that they were confused. I tried to guide them to figure it out for themselves, but that was met with frustration and confusion. In my journal I referred to how classroom management was a disaster that day. "Water was spilling, students were eating, and

I think there was a craps game in the corner when my back was turned." I do not really remember a craps game though, so I think that last part was written in frustration.

Early in the lab, students were asked to find the weight of an object, but the scale they were using read mass.[2] Unaware that they needed to make a conversion on their own, I reminded them that they should have been familiar with the relationship between the two.[3] They should have seen the simple equation hundreds of times in the previous three months. Regardless, they wanted a reference table without trying to figure it out or even just remember.

There was another problem, one involving the rather simple conversion of grams to kilograms. Every student had been doing this kind of conversion for years. I reviewed how to do the straight forward calculation again early in the lab. Still there was confusion.

One lab group was especially frustrated. I had already worked through multiple examples of conversion so I eventually directed this group to work the next one out on their own. Table spokesperson George, a poor student by any measure, expressed his feeling in his own typical way:

How am I supposed to do if you don't tell me? Hey Phil (across the room), go build a rocket but I'm not going to tell you how.

There was no expectation by George and so many other students that they should apply or build on what they already knew. They wanted to be told what to do each time. Sure, I showed them how to do the conversion with one value, but the group was now being asked to do it with a different value.

For so many students, learning was about doing exactly what you are told or repeating back something given by some authority. Understanding something well enough to do it on your own was rarely a student goal.

Not one group was able to complete the lab successfully in the first section with which I implemented it, but I was persistent. I made some modifications to the write-up. I also think some practice on my part made a difference. Late in the week in my period 4 lab section, most of the students were working well and were on task. They even got the point of trying to figure things out for themselves.

Kimi: *How do I do this?* (Measure apparent mass of a submerged object.)

Me: *You have to figure it out.*

Julia: *I told you that he was going to say that.*

---

[2] The difference between weight (measured in Newtons or pounds) and mass (measured in grams or kilograms) is just a multiplicative constant.

[3] $W = mg$.

After leaving the group with only giving some minor guidance, they then worked constructively on their own. Neither this group nor any other was engaged in a craps game.

TELL THEM THEN ASSESS THEM

I was talking to an Assistant Principal at one of my regular Professional Development meetings. I had known him for several years and had great respect for him. I was eager to ask him about how to be a better teacher. He did not hesitate about what he wanted to share first. The kids need to know what they are going to be tested on. "How are they supposed to know what they have to learn if we don't tell them?"

It sounded so reasonable, but it reminded me of Mr. Lowrey who started the year with going over old Regents exams. Learning needs to be about making sense of the world. Learning needs to be about inquiring into meaningful, fruitful areas of interest in which development of skills happens naturally. Learning needs to be about asking questions and then coming up with strategies to answer those questions.

Nowhere are these approaches to learning more important than in science. Instead, learning science in school was (de facto) about being told what you were going to have to know ahead of time and then repeating it back on command. We are training students to expect to be told.

WHO'S THE AUTHORITY?

There were many days I was not sure who was training whom. After a unit on angular motion, I was particularly disappointed with student exam performance. The questions on the exam were very similar to what was explicitly covered in class. It was material I was certain that they had the ability to answer. These were quantitative problems with mathematics that they could execute.

After returning the exams, I went through the solutions during class showing them exactly how to do each step. To ensure that they understood, and to give them an opportunity to improve their grades, I told them that there would be a quiz identical to the exam except I would just change the numerical values of the problems from what was just gone over. They would then just need to do exactly what I just went over using different numbers.

Regardless, there was an uproar that the quiz would therefore *not* be the same. I relented and told them I would tell them exactly what the questions would be and how to solve them before giving the quiz. This was not the approach that I intended to take when I signed up to teach at UHS.

MR. AGEE AND NATE

Mr. Agee was a science teacher down the hall who had been at UHS for about five years. He struck me as a quiet, competent man who had a solid rapport with the students.

As part of my routine, I went to observe Mr. Agee. He was conducting a lesson on the parts of a cell. He went through a worksheet with short answer questions about the topic. Students were called on to answer each question receiving small rewards when answering correctly and small punishments when answering incorrectly. (There was some kind of point system which factored into their grades that I did not quite understand, but Mr. Agee's students did.)

Questions were easy to understand and answers were spelled out clearly in the chapter. Most students were able to answer correctly, regardless of whether they had a meaningful understanding of the words they were stating. The pace was quick. With points at stake and questions flying, classroom management seemed to not be a problem. With a high percentage of questions answered correctly, there was the appearance that the lesson was effective. I was concerned that it was effective at the wrong things.

Nate was a student in one of my Regents Physics classes. He was bright, but like most of my students he did not know how to go about learning physics. He was also more than an occasional challenge behaviorally.

After observing Mr. Agee, I recalled an exchange with Nate early in the year that was a concern at the time. It was also a concern all year with many of my students. Nate was working on a problem about motion in one dimension. It was certainly something that he could do, even though the problem was somewhat involved, but he gave up and wanted help from me less than one minute in. The reason that he gave me was that the problem was "too long."

I know that Nate could have worked intelligently to solve this problem on his own or with his classmates around him. Unfortunately, stretching to work though a challenging problem independently was not part of Nate's world view. Despite encouragement and guidance from me, Nate switched to mischief instead.

I could only speculate that Nate probably would have done well in Mr. Agee's class.

BUT THAT WAS IN SEPTEMBER

In Regents Physics we were covering electricity phenomena. For the Regents curriculum, that included Coulomb's law, electric fields, and superposition. There was a quiz coming up, and I reminded the students (as I often did) that all quizzes were cumulative from the beginning of the year.

Islam called out "How am I supposed to remember what we did in September?" All I could think was "How can you understand electrical forces without understanding forces? How can you make sense of electric fields without building on gravitational fields? How can you apply the principal of superposition without understanding vectors?"

There was no expectation that knowledge, learning, and understanding were cumulative. Islam, and so many others, thought of knowledge as pieces of information to be presented by the teacher, and then memorized, repeated, and forgotten by the student.

SOMEONE ELSE'S REASONING

One strategy that I kept trying, with some success, was to have students analyze someone else's reasoning about a science problem. I would present a problem where I knew students would not agree on an answer. Students needed to state the answer to the problem and how they came up with that answer. But that was not enough. They had to determine what was wrong with a classmate's reasoning which was used to support a different answer.

Students needed to explain, justify, interpret, and negotiate the underlying concepts and strategies associated with the problem. They needed to articulate their own reasoning in a way that others could understand and find a hole in the reasoning of someone else who came up with a different answer.

For example, after studying circuits, I drew the circuit shown in Figure 6.1 on the board. Students were asked to rank the voltages across the six bulbs with the switch between A and B open. Two of my stronger students came to a disagreement. Rosa said that bulb B would be zero volts because it was not lit. Jose said that B would have half of bulb C's voltage because the voltage of A and B must add up to the voltage of C.

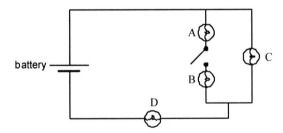

Figure 6.1. Circuit diagram used to facilitate students negotiating different reasoning.

I told Rosa and Jose that they both presented good arguments. I asked them each to find a hole in the other's reasoning. Instead, what they each did was repeat their own argument louder and slower. That did not seem to change anyone's mind.

Usually it takes some time and some guidance from me to redirect a conversation like this to one where everyone recognizes the flaw in one or both arguments and work towards a consensus answer.[4] On this particular day though, I inadvertently gave away the correct answer before the negotiation. The class was amused and not interested in my attempts to hide my gaffe. We discussed the problem and the reasoning of both answers and most of the class seemed to understand the problem. Sometimes an accidental strategy works too.

IT'S CIRCULAR REASONING BECAUSE IT'S CIRCULAR REASONING

Eventually it was no surprise to my students that I had higher aspirations than them just knowing science facts. For example, one priority was having students know how we know what we know.

Even before getting to the unit on light, most of my students were familiar with the fact that if you shine white light through a prism, you see light of different colors come out the other side. I did not go through this to remind them of the outcome of this particular experiment. I wanted my students to think about how scientific knowledge is developed.

Ledell: *If you shine the light through the prism, you will get different colors on the other side because white light is made up of different colors.*

That sounds good. The comment is intelligent and relevant. But the underlying reasoning is worth exploring.

Me: *How do you know white light is made up of different colors?*

Ledell: *Because if you shine white light through the prism you will get different colors?*

Me: *How do you know if you shine white light through the prism you will get different colors?*

Ledell: *Because white light is made up of different colors.*

The problem with this line of reasoning might be subtle, but it is important. I do not want students to simultaneously justify knowing the outcome of the experiment because of the properties of light while justifying knowing the properties of light because of the outcome of the experiment. Scientific knowledge is something that can be constructed logically from observations and reasoning, not something to be taken on faith because of the mandate of some unknown (or known) authority.

---

[4] In this case, Rosa was correct. Jose's reasoning was incorrect because he did not account for the voltage across the switch.

With some effort on my part, but NOT because of any edict from me, I tried to get my students to see the difference. We *observe* that white light that shines through a prism comes out different colors. From this observation (and others) we *infer* that white light is made up of different colors.

REFLECTIONS ON INDEPENDENCE OF LEARNING

When teaching, I always struggle with trying to prioritize the importance of independent learning even though I am nominally the authority in the room. But it seems to me that if students are to be real learners of science, they must take responsibility of coming to understand the material for themselves. It is the only way that I have seen science learned properly. It is the only way that I can imagine students having a real understanding of what science is. Sure, the teacher needs be there to define the class and provide lots of guidance, help, support, ideas, and even answers. However, the students need to take charge of making sense of it for themselves. Otherwise it is just a bunch of someone else's unprocessed words.

Furthermore, if one is to go on to advanced learning of science and careers in science and related fields, it is a necessary skill to be able to learn, think, and take responsibility. It is necessary to be able to solve problems different from any other problem encountered before. Few professionals are hired to grind mindlessly through steps that a computer can execute. Come to think of it, I think these are all good reasons for those who are not going on to more advanced learning of science to approach learning science this way too.

STRATEGIES THAT WORK: INDEPENDENT LEARNING

Learning how to think independently, learning how to ask questions and pursue answers, learning how to develop problem solving strategies, and learning how to learn should all be important outcomes of a good education. I struggle to see how these skills are given enough priority in schools today. There are however strategies that address them, some of which have been described already.

Lab should be a wonderful context to develop independent learning skills. I met with mixed success when I broke from the traditional "cook-book" lab approach and had students take more responsibility.[5] But I did see enough good things happen to be optimistic. Many places, including the University of Maryland, have successfully developed labs which are much more student directed.[6] Real world problems are presented and students ask questions, design and carry out experiments, and interpret real results. Students work towards the learning goals described above. They also learn the science content along the way.

---

[5]   I met with less than mixed success when I didn't break from the traditional cook-book lab approach.

[6]   For a description of the approach, handouts, and research of the student centered labs developed by the University of Maryland Physics Education Research Group, see www.physics.umd.edu/perg.

Of course independent learning activities should not be limited to the lab. Two other examples are listed below. The first is question related to the behavior of white light passing through a prism. Students struggle with identifying how one comes to know a scientific idea. While productive, the dialogue about white light going through a prism described earlier in this chapter is limited. I therefore have students follow up by writing about it. Here they must explicitly delineate what is known and how it has come to be known. Both quotes written below might be correct, but the difference between them is critical, and often lost on the students without some help.

The second example is an essay about scientific literacy. It is intended to be asked after finishing an astronomy class similar to the one described in for the Summer Scholars Program. In practice, students who write this essay share meaningful perspectives critical of the notion that scientific knowledge could be equated with identification of pieces of information. They also often share that there is more to understanding that the earth goes around the sun than a simple statement to that effect from a teacher.

Compare and contrast word problem about light

Compare and contrast the reasoning of the following 2 statements made by different students:

Student 1: *"If you shine white light through a prism, you see different colors come out the other side because white light is made up of light of different colors."*

Student 2: *"When you shine white light through a prism, you see different colors come out the other side. From this you can infer that white light might be made up of different colors."*

Essay given as exam question

New York Times published an article on scientific illiteracy in the United States. The article noted, "Nearly 500 years after Copernicus postulated that the earth revolves around the sun, millions of Americans say otherwise ... 95% of those polled were ignorant of basic and simple scientific facts and had to be considered scientifically illiterate ... 21% of those questioned were of the opinion that the sun revolved around the earth and an additional 7% didn't know which went around which." The article concluded that: "How can any teacher, however poorly prepared, not teach that the earth goes around the sun?"

Write an essay detailing your perspective of this position. In particular, make reference to the appropriateness of what was used to measure minimum scientific literacy. Also, describe your perspective of the implied pedagogy.

CHAPTER 6

LEONARDO DA VINCI

That students have such difficulty remembering what they were told by their teachers is often noted with great concern. That the goal is to have students simply remember what they were told concerns me more. I interpret the statement by da Vinci about intellect and memory as the need for education to highlight much more than the capacity to remember what one has been told. Schooling needs to refocus on developing the capacity to know how we know, to reason intelligently, to explain clearly, and to negotiate intellectually. And as far as I am concerned, if da Vinci says so, that is good enough for me.

LEO SAYS GER

Assessment

One had to cram all this stuff into one's mind for the examinations, whether one liked it or not. This coercion had such a deterring effect on me that, after I had passed the final examination, I found the consideration of any scientific problems distasteful to me for an entire year.

Not everything that counts can be counted, and not everything that can be counted counts.

  - Albert Einstein

JANUARY 28: LEARNING CHEMISTRY (IDEAL VACATIONS ARE BAD)

Takoa Lawson was my colleague in the Summer Scholars Program the summer before sabbatical. He was also a wonderful high school science chemistry teacher while I was on sabbatical, although at a different school. Takoa has always been a dedicated and caring teacher. He works hard to do the best for his students. I have always admired the way he constantly tries to improve his own understanding of both science and teaching. He also cares deeply that the learning of his students is real. As an experienced high school teacher, he knows and has seen a lot.

One frustrating day in January, I shared my concerns[1] with Takoa about preparing my students for a test that covered too much material and did not emphasize the many reasoning and process skills that I valued most. He described to me some of the strategies that other teachers used to get students to succeed on the chemistry Regents, even though they were strategies he would not use himself. He told me about "Leo says ger." Students use this as a mnemonic to remember how to answer oxidation and reduction problems without understanding oxidation and reduction.[2] That was interesting, but I was more entertained when he told me "An ideal vacation is a hot place with low pressure from your parents."

The Ideal Gas Law is part of the curriculum of Regents chemistry. This is a good thing. After all, thinking of gas as a collection of spread out particles behaving in a particular way is fundamental to understanding a great deal of scientific phenomena. Furthermore, the kinetic theory of gasses is a wonderful place to practice the very kind of scientific activities and reasoning that I argue for

---

[1] Read "whined."

[2] The l and g are for lose and gain, the e is for electron, and the o and r are for oxidation and reduction.

throughout this book. What are our observations of gasses? How can we make sense of them? How can we relate them to what we have learned about the way gasses combine? How can we develop and build a scientific model that accounts for everything we see and know?

For the chemistry Regents, students are expected to know how and when real gasses differ from ideal. They should learn about how the volume of a real gas molecule becomes more significant when the pressure is greater. At higher pressure the molecules are closer together. They should learn about how the interaction forces between real gas molecules become more significant when the temperature is lower. At lower temperatures the molecules are moving more slowly. It takes real understanding of the kinetic theory of gasses to intelligently identify these limitations of the Ideal Gas Law.

However, many students instead just remember that (apparently) an ideal vacation is in a hot place with low pressure from your parents. Students are taught explicitly that when you see a question about an "ideal" gas to just remember that it is more ideal if you have a "high temperature" and "low pressure." Hence, the mnemonic yields the correct result. There is no need to understand why it is the way it is. Science has been reduced to something very unscientific.

There are instructors who explicitly tell their students the strategy about ideal vacations in anticipation of being asked the following typical chemistry Regents question:

Under which conditions of temperature and pressure does oxygen gas behave least like an ideal gas?[3]

(1) low temperature and low pressure

(2) low temperature and high pressure

(3) high temperature and low pressure

(4) high temperature and high pressure

Social commentary about vacationing aside, I have a real problem with this very non-ideal way of test preparation in chemistry. In testing for student understanding of gasses, students have come up with a strategy to answer the question correctly regardless of any understanding of gasses. Their success on answering this question is irrelevant to anything meaningful with respect to knowing science. Even worse, students are left with a disposition that understanding science correlates with an approach that has nothing to do with scientific thinking. (There seems to be a pattern with this.)

---

[3] I am not sure of the purpose of the "least" in this particular Regents question other than to see if test takers are reading the question carefully.

WHAT ABOUT PHYSICS?

I was obviously worried about how my students were going to do on the physics Regents. The system and students alike put pressure on me to prepare them for this particular test. All year I studied old physics Regents questions to get a sense of what was expected. As a result, part of me felt that if I could get them to understand the material they would be able to answer many of the questions correctly. The problem was that it would be arduous and time consuming for each area of content required. There were a lot of content areas.

Unfortunately I recognized that students might find it much easier, and probably more strategic, to take a different approach. Some Regents questions called for knowing how to eliminate choices for a half-understood definition of a technical term. Other questions were so predictable that I could just show them how to answer those specific questions. For so many questions though, it was probably best to teach the students to just find a relevant looking equation on the reference table.

A typical example of a question that students could answer regardless of whether they understood it is:

What is the resistance at 20.°C of a 2.0-meter length of tungsten wire with a cross-sectional area of 7.9×10^{-7} meter²?

    (1) 5.7 x 10^{-1} Ω   *(3) 7.1 x 10^{-2} Ω*

    (2) 1.4 x 10^{-1} Ω   *(4) 4.0 x 10^{-2} Ω*

I had a lot of confidence that at the end of the year that my students would have limited understanding of resistance and resistivity. The relevance of temperature and metal dependence of resistivity were out of the question. However, the formula for resistivity might be accessible. There was only one formula that had resistivity in it on the reference table. There was so little time for each topic. An approach that I could have taken was to try to get students to know how to use the equation. I said to myself "I don't care, I won't do it!" At least that was the disposition that I tried to maintain.

Lisa was one of my best and most engaged students. She was very successful, scoring high marks on homework and exams routinely. Despite this success, her epistemological approaches were not that great. She focused on surface features, jargon, and formulas much more than on big ideas, concepts, and understanding what the physics was about. Regardless, she always came to class with a smile, willing and eager to learn.

While reviewing in class for the Regents, when I got to the resistance question above I relented and showed everyone how to use the reference table to answer it. Lisa said "I don't understand." Spontaneously, I replied "You don't have to understand. Just use the reference table and plug the numbers into the formula." Later in the class Lisa complained "This is boring." My journal entry that day about this exchange is stained with tear marks.

In fairness to the physics Regents, there were other questions which could not be answered with these kinds of strategies so easily. What is the corresponding graph for different motions? What happens as different objects collide in different ways? However, these questions were in the minority. The pace of the material taught and the nature of the majority of the questions dictated the personality of the course. It was not a personality that I liked.

I came to appreciate why so many of my college students came to my college classes with such poor epistemological approaches and weak understanding of physics content. And no wonder I was feeling so stressed trying to teach real physics while simultaneously trying to prepare my students for the Regents.

WHAT ABOUT EARTH SCIENCE?

Like the other teachers at UHS, one of my responsibilities was to proctor Regents exams in the other subject areas. During mid-year testing week I got to look at other exams that students took, including the earth science Regents. The curricula in earth science include the motion of the sun, earth, moon, and planets. That meant I got to see questions about the same curricula that I covered in the Summer Scholars Program.

There were a few questions that attempted to probe for reasoning in this context. One question asked students to consider what evidence about the earth the Coriolis Effect provides. But I am not sure if students tried to understand underlying ideas or memorize their way through questions like these.

Regardless, most of the astronomy questions were about facts and numbers on topics beyond the scope that high school students could hope to have insight into. What is the age of the universe? Is the star Algol classified as a main sequence star, red giant star, dwarf star, or ninja star[4]?

One question that caught my eye in particular was:

As viewed from Earth, most stars appear to move across the sky each night because:

    (1) Earth revolves around the Sun

    (2) Earth rotates on its axis

    (3) stars orbit around Earth

    (4) stars revolve around the center of the galaxy

My former Summer Scholars might very well have taken this very Regents test and answered this very question with (3). Or maybe they wrote in "I don't know." This might not be considered correct by the graders, but I don't feel guilty. I know that my former students' scientific reasoning is strong. I know that their thinking about the topic is sophisticated and meaningful.

---

[4]   It didn't really say ninja star, but it might as well have.

WHAT ABOUT MATH?

I didn't see fundamental differences among the Regents exam questions in the different sciences. Unfortunately I saw how most of these questions could result in students taking a Leo says Ger approach to preparing for their test. This got me to thinking about math.

I saw so many difficulties that students had applying basic math in my physics classes. In an earlier chapter I wrote how I wanted my students to come into physics with a stronger foundation in math. I respectfully noted[5] that tests need to assure that these skills are in place and kids need to succeed on these kinds of tests. What did the math Regents questions look like?

When I looked at some math Regents exams, I saw that there were questions on volume calculations, probability, algebra, and functions. These questions correspond to appropriate expectations. These are skills that I want my students to have in my high school physics class. I recognize how students could work towards deep and meaningful understanding of concepts and ideas to learn how to answer them. I also recognize how students could be drilled on de-contextualized procedures to learn how to answer them. In practice, I saw more of the latter than the former.

This led me to think about inquiry, a real theme in the way I was trying to teach my science classes. Math too is such a wonderful subject where one can learn by and about inquiry, but somehow it felt different than science. Maybe there is a little science snob in me, but science feels like *the* place to learn inquiry. There are so many things a student can see, hear, feel, smell, taste and explore in science. There are so many fun science things that define the world around us. There are so many opportunities to reason, test, measure, and experiment.

Teaching physics also got me to realize that another fundamental difference between math and science is related to preparation for subsequent work. I needed my students to be able to know about volume calculations, probability, algebra, and functions.[6] I don't think math teachers needed students to know about neutrinos, decay modes of radioactive isotopes, or eccentricity of the planets' elliptical motion.

I got to thinking about other ways that math and science are not the same.

There is a base level of both math and science content knowledge that all students should have, but it is clearer for math what that should be. I would rather have my science students have deep understanding of a subset of science topics even if they miss some topics altogether. The content in which they learn scientific reasoning and process skills is less important than them having these skills. After studying math, I want all of my students to know how to take an average and construct a graph.

There are specific skills which students should have after completing both math and science, but it is easier to test for those skills in math. I was not impressed with much of the math instruction that I saw or student abilities to apply mathematics

---

[5]   Read "whined."

[6]   They didn't.

knowledge in my science class. However it seems like testing for basic math content well is more realistic than testing for basic science content well.

There are opportunities to exercise and develop reasoning, process, and inquiry skills in both math and science, but science is really the most wonderful place to do this. (I guess there is more than just a little science snob in me.) Developing thinking skills in school is at least as important as developing mastery in mathematical tools. *Both* are critical. Neither is much good without the other. Fortunately, developing good thinking skills can (and should) go hand in hand with developing mastery with mathematical tools.

THE MENTALITY OF HYPER-ASSESSMENT

Throughout the school year while teaching at UHS, I continued to attend teacher education classes in the evenings as a student. Here is a journal entry that I wrote after one of my January classes.

> *We talked about assessment in my class tonight. There is such emphasis on assessing for that which could be clearly and reliably assessed. I can't help but worry that this will cause the omission of many of those skills which are of greatest importance but which are not as easily tested for.*

This was on my mind a great deal in the way my Regents physics class was playing out. Testing for vocabulary and formulas is easy. You know it or you don't. Writing these kinds of questions is clear and easy. Grading these kinds of questions is unambiguous and simple.

Testing for reasoning and scientific process is hard.[7] These skills emerge slowly and unevenly. Writing these kinds of questions is subtle and hard. Grading these kinds of questions is ambiguous and challenging.

I was troubled. What is the solution to the conflict that many of the things that students should learn in science that are of greatest value are those that are hardest to assess? I was frustrated in my preparing students so hard for an exam which had become so much about questions on jargon and formulas. It was hardly at all about reasoning and process. There must be accountability, but accountability about lots of different things, especially those things that are most important.

There was more. I was troubled by what I saw as a mentality of hyper-assessment. When it was all about the test, it was all about the test – for students, teachers, and administrators. When it was all about things that can be easily tested, it was all about things that can be easily tested – for students, teachers, and administrators.

What to think was more important than how to think. Content was primary, process and reasoning were secondary. Intellectual obedience was more important

---

[7]   Reasoning and scientific process skills should *not* be developed or assessed devoid of content. The context for learning and assessing reasoning and process should be in specific content. This is the best way to teach and assess reasoning, process, and content.

than intellectual curiosity. Pieces of information were more important than big ideas. Students approached learning by memorizing more than by understanding. Prescription was more important than creativity. Having to learn was the norm, loving to learn was the exception. Uniformity in teaching was more important than innovation and passion.

An inevitable consequence of this mentality of hyper-assessment was the marginalization of the arts and sciences. Ironically this resulted in a lost opportunity to leverage context and desire to improve the very skills that were being tested for.

An inevitable consequence of this mentality of hyper-assessment was the frustration of the very best teachers that I saw. Tragically, this resulted in so many of them looking to other career paths.

NO CHILD LEFT BEHIND?

Even though my schedule and workload were overwhelming, I chose to attend a seminar on No Child Left Behind (NCLB) at a nearby college one wintery day. There I was, right back in the ivory tower,[8] but this time with a different vantage. I recognized NCLB[9] as a controversial topic that was oft debated in books, editorial pages, colleges of education, and sports bars everywhere. Opinions are strong and varied. Mine was dominated at the time by what was related to me being a new science teacher in a tough urban high school.

Not surprisingly, the seminar began by citing calls for "accountability" and "standards." Who can argue with that? I have never met anyone who said "we need schools to be less accountable" or "I am against academic standards." I wish NCLB's call for accountability and standards ended the parade of students like those in my classes who lacked the preparation that they should have had by that point in their schooling.

Then I heard a lot about math and literacy. There were compelling statistics and persuasive arguments noting how scores on math and literacy tests correlated with eventual success in college and beyond. But correlations are notoriously difficult to interpret. Just for the record, I am completely pro math and literacy education, but as an educator I want so much more. My students did not have the math or literacy skills that I wanted them to have, but this was only a piece of the story. These skills are necessary, but very far from sufficient.

Whether I was teaching a struggling eleventh grader or a high achieving college senior, I saw bigger deficits in epistemological approaches and reasoning abilities than in math and literacy skills. I also saw math and literacy acumen used to mask deficits in other important areas. It is dubious to believe that training students to

---

[8] I talk about being "away" from the ivory tower rather than "down" from it because I feel strongly that my work and disposition are not that of being above anything. (I also try to never be "away" from anything, but I am not in the public schools when I teach at the college.) Even if not universal, many of my colleagues feel the same.

[9] Subsequent national policies under different banners than "No Child Left Behind" are strikingly similar.

pass math and literacy tests at the expense of all of the other critical skills is in their best interest, regardless of the outcome of those very tests.

Discussed most though at the seminar was the thing that always gets the most attention: the testing. Lots and lots of testing with lots and lots of consequences based on the results. Testing is good. We need students (and teachers and schools) to be successful and we need this to be documented. But given my experience at UHS, lots and lots of testing with lots and lots of consequences based on the results was a red flag.[10] At UHS (and most other high schools) it was all about the tests and the results. I was not impressed with how that played out.

Throughout the seminar I was concerned that the focus on testing exacerbates an emphasis on that which is easily assessed. This is a problem. A lot of smart, dedicated, highly competent physics educators have worked on the development of the physics Regents dating back to before 1982 (when I took it). After all of those years, the physics Regents is an exam students approach by looking up formulas, memorizing vocabulary, or thinking about vacations without their parents. Furthermore, I am guessing that tests that satisfy psychometricians most are tests that satisfy me least.[11]

I was also concerned that as the consequences of the testing increase, the mentality of hyper-assessment grows. The stakes are high. Schools can be graded poorly or shut down. Principals' jobs and budgets can be on the line. And of course everyone loves to debate about whether teachers' salaries should be tied to student scores.

Lest I forget, one way or another, the students are the ones with the most on the line in the world of high stakes testing. They are not oblivious to it. With raised stakes, all of the concerns about lots and lots of testing amplify. This worries me because so many of the difficulties that I saw at UHS were tied to the culture of it being all about the test.

The seminar led me to consider so many potential pitfalls when it is all about the test. Would schools having great success with innovative learning programs need to make adjustments to a more standard curricula and testing approach? Would charter schools be motivated to target enrollment to students most likely to score high (or achieve large gains)? Would test driven schools populated with students bound for elite colleges move even further to the mentality of hyper-assessment and rigid curricula? (I couldn't help but think about the mentality that my Summer Scholars Students entered my program with each summer.) Would school systems find reasons to steer weaker students away from the more challenging classes? Would the "high stakes" in high stakes testing lead to rampant cheating, unethical student enrollment procedures, and nefarious institutional practices?[12]

But it was clear to me that students and schools with the lowest test scores have the most to worry about. This is despite the fact that there are a myriad of complex

---

[10] Later that became a white flag for me.
[11] Statistically significant is not the same as significant!
[12] The answers to all of these questions turns out to be very much "yes."

reasons that the scores are low, many of which have nothing to do with what is going on in the school. These schools need to pay the most attention to the test. If that does not work, than they need to make changes to make success on the tests an even higher priority. But what if the culture of the test is in conflict to meaningful learning? What if focusing on short-term improvement on these tests has the long-term cost of poor preparedness for real success? Then the kids that are in most need are the ones being left behind the most.

Not surprisingly, on the panel at the seminar were those that presented themselves as either for or against NCLB, particularly the testing. Those that were for NCLB predictably described the need for quantitative data and accountability. Results of test scores were presented as an argument that the results of test scores are of value. Without a great deal more support, this seemed to me just like the circular reasoning that I kept seeing in my high school classes.

Those that were critical of NCLB focused on cultural bias, student affect, and financial limitations accounting for low scores by particular demographics. Therefore even those critical of testing as constituted seemed to ignore the dangers that worried me the most. As I watched the debate, for some reason I felt like the child who saw the emperor without any clothes. Why was no one saying anything?

NO TEACHER LEFT ALONE!

Each month at UHS there were multiple professional development and/or staff meetings. Many of these were kicked off by the principal. One such session began with him stating "Big Brother is coming." He told us that there will be many new assessments, "school by school, teacher by teacher, and student by student."

The meaning was clear. It was consistent with national trends at all levels. Expect rigorous testing and expect that the results of this testing will be strictly interpreted to gauge the intelligence of the student, the quality of the teacher, and the success of the school. This means large databases, multiple-choice tests, and rigid curricula.

The meaning was clear. If 82% of my students could answer a question about what a Tau neutrino was, that would be good. If half of my students did not know whether the earth went around the sun or if the sun went around the earth, that would be bad.

The manner in which the principal stressed his big brother comment was also clear. Everything that all of us teachers were going to do would be built around what was needed to get our students to succeed on the tests.

THAT'S JUST NOT FAIR

I knew that the standardized test questions that my students would take were vetted with an extended process of field testing and statistical analysis. One criterion used to determine whether a new question is reliable is to see if higher scoring students throughout the state answer the question correctly at a high enough rate. If not, the question might be thrown out and not used. Another criterion is that overall student success rate needs to be high enough. If not, the question might be thrown out and not used. There are good reasons for doing this. Regardless, before sabbatical this used to bother me. While teaching at UHS it bothered me more.

For example, suppose that there are new questions under development which probe student ability to connect classroom learning with real world experiences. It could be that some of these questions give low scoring inner city students a statistically higher chance to answer correctly than high scoring students state-wide. Maybe it is a geology question related to rock folds visible in Central Park. Maybe it is a question about rectilinear coordinates that resembles city streets. If these questions are answered less well by students with tutors training them with Leo says ger approaches, there is risk that they could be discarded as undependable. This is not just a cultural bias, it is an epistemological bias. There is a bias against implementing questions which encourage epistemological approaches which differ from those of the majority, even if the epistemological approaches of the majority are poor.

As another example, suppose there are new questions about scientific reasoning under development, very different from existing questions. It is likely that these questions would result in small percentages of students answering correctly. Teachers who focus on depth of understanding and critical thinking skills might have students do better on these questions than students with other teachers. Too bad these questions might not survive. They would not be discriminating enough if too many students answer incorrectly throughout the state. Furthermore, which students are doing well might not fit the desired profile. Even worse though, if we include questions students struggle greatly with, it would create the perception that the schools are failing. Focusing on questions which are easier to train students to answer correctly is an easier way to get scores up. The perception of learning is valued more than the reality of learning.

The system is functionally set up to propagate the lowest common denominator. But educators are the system. It does not have to be this way.

REGENTS FREE ZONE: GOOD, BUT NOT ALWAYS A HAPPY ENDING

I shared some of my concerns about the impact of the Regents on my experience at UHS with my CCNY colleague Greg Borman. He told me about a small subset of students who go through high school with less Regents pressure in schools that have a Regents waiver. Student experiences at these schools are diverse, but overall there is less emphasis on covering broad content and more emphasis on depth of understanding. There is less traditional instruction and more student-directed work and project based curricula. He described how for the most part, learning for these students is much better than in schools without a Regents waiver. All I could think was "Where do I sign up?"

Unfortunately, Greg also shared with me feedback from some of these students after going to college. Students who had a less test-prep based high school experience often had a hard time in college for all the wrong reasons. They were unfamiliar with the textbook-focused, fact-based implementations of most college introductory lecture classes. They struggled with predominantly passive learning environments. They needed to adjust to processing large amounts of barely comprehensible material. As a college professor, I recognize that students from ALL high schools struggle with these same issues when they get to college, but it must be especially unfortunate for those from more enriching high school experiences.

Based on my knowledge of a great number of traditional college classes across the country, this feedback is not surprising, even though it is disappointing.

MORE FROM MY EDUCATION CLASSES: IDEAL VACATIONS ARE IRRELEVANT

As part of my enrollment in a teacher education program I learned a little about what other countries do, which felt different than what I was experiencing as a new teacher at UHS. For example, there are places where teachers are treated as respected professionals who need to work towards being experts in their craft. These teachers are given support and opportunity to learn and implement a real inquiry approach to classroom practice. Curricula at all levels are more focused on critical thinking skills and less on the kind of rote skills practiced when it is all about the test.

Along the way students in these countries out-perform students in this country on tests. I doubt that in any of these countries that they teach about ideal vacations being hot and parent-free.

REFLECTIONS ON TESTING

Testing students is necessary. Students must demonstrate knowledge and skills. Schools need standards and need to be accountable. But my students were immersed in an extreme culture of testing. Regardless of intentions, this resulted in a situation with dire educational consequences. The way they prepared for the tests created a flawed approach to learning, weak retention of content knowledge, poor epistemological skills, limited ability to transfer knowledge, and a general lack of preparedness for success outside of the classroom. Specific examples cited in this chapter were from New York State high school science Regents exams and curricula. However, there is every reason to think that this is not idiosyncratic.

We need to test, but we need to be sure that the tests assess the diversity of what we care about. Test results need to count, but we need to be sure not to create a culture which adversely changes the mentality of the student and teacher. The stakes could be high if we fail to test. However, detailed perspective from where the rubber hits the road has shown me that the stakes are higher if we do it wrong... and we are doing it wrong.

STRATEGIES THAT WORK: ASSESSMENT

The majority of science questions that I have seen on standardized exams focus on recall of information, regardless of whether there is understanding of what is being recalled. However there are many exceptions. Some are multiple-choice, some are short answer, some are numeric problems, and some are something else. Strategies that work do exist. Here I describe some strategies with multiple-choice questions.

Research into the development of multiple-choice conceptual test questions has been done in many topics including astronomy,[13] biology,[14] natural selection,[15] motion graphs,[16] forces,[17] electricity and magnetism,[18] circuits,[19] and scientific reasoning.[20] These tests were primarily intended for use as diagnostics and not as classroom tests, but there is much that can be learned about testing that does not focus on simply recall.

In my classes, I have used multiple-choice questions on exams which have the goal to focus more on conceptual thinking. Some are traditional multiple-choice format. Some require students to explain their reasoning. Some require students to potentially select more than one correct answer. Some require students to determine if any of the choices make sense. Below, I share examples in a variety of science topics.

[13] www.cis.rit.edu/~jnspci/AAE/adt.shtml

[14] Garvin-Doxas, K., & Klymkowsky, M. W. (2008). Understanding randomness and its impact on student learning: Lessons learned from building the Biology Concept Inventory (BCI). *Life Sciences Education, 7.*

[15] Anderson, D. L., Fisher, K. M., & Norman, G. J. (2002). Development and evaluation of the conceptual inventory of natural selection. *J. Res. Sci. Teach., 39,* 10.

[16] Beichner, R. (1994). Testing student interpretation of kinematics graphs. *The American Journal of Physics, 62.*

[17] Hestenes, D., Wells, M., & Swackhammer, G. (1992). Force concept inventory. *Phys. Teach., 30.*

[18] Maloney, D., O'Kuma, T., Hieggelke, C., & Van Heuvelen, A. (2001). Surveying students' conceptual knowledge of electricity and magnetism. *The American Journal of Physics, 69.*

[19] Engelhardt, P., & Beichner, R. (2004). Students' understanding of direct current resistive electrical circuits. *The American Journal of Physics, 72*

[20] Lawson, A. E. (1978). Classroom test of scientific reasoning. *J. Res. Sci. Teach., 15,* 11

Conceptual multiple-choice questions

The circuit shown at right contains 5 identical bulbs labeled A-E. (Assume that the battery, wires, and switch are ideal.)

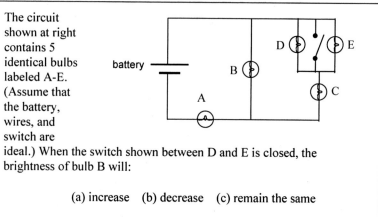

When the switch shown between D and E is closed, the brightness of bulb B will:

(a) increase   (b) decrease   (c) remain the same

A container of water is placed on a scale which reads 100 N as shown in figure (a) at right. A 25 N metal block supported by a string is then placed into the water as shown in figure (b) at right. The object is at rest and does not touch the sides or bottom of the container at all. The reading on the scale is:

(a)   Less than 75 N

(b)   Exactly 75 N

(c)   Between 75 N and 100 N

(d)   Exactly 100 N

(e)   Between 100 N and 125 N

(f)   Exactly 125 N

(g)   More than 125 N

A person attempts to knock down a large bowling pin by throwing a ball at it. The person has 2 balls of equal size, shape, and mass, one made of rubber and the other of putty. The rubber ball bounces back, while the ball of putty sticks to the pin. Which ball is more likely to knock down the bowling pin?

(a) The rubber ball (b) The ball of putty (c) It makes no difference

Explain your reasoning.

Consider a small boat floating in a tank of water. Resting on the boat is a large piece of Styrofoam. (See figure at right.) When the Styrofoam falls off the boat and lands in the water, which of the following applies? *Circle ALL that apply.*

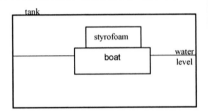

(a) The level of the water against the side of the tank goes up.

(b) The level of the water against the side of the tank goes down.

(c) The level of the water against the side of the tank stays the same.

(d) The level of the water against the side of the boat is higher.

(e) The level of the water against the side of the boat is lower.

(f) The level of the water against the side of the boat is the same.

A hand holds one side of a long taut string which is attached to a distant wall at the other side. The hand moves in a way that creates a small amplitude pulse which travels down the string and reaches the wall in a time t_0. A small red dot is painted on the string halfway between the hand and the wall. For each question below left, state which actions a-k listed below right **taken by itself** will produce the desired result. *List ALL that apply.*[21]

How, if at all, can a demonstrator repeat the original experiment to produce:

A pulse that takes a longer time to reach the wall.
Action(s):_____

A pulse that is wider than the original pulse.
Action(s):_____

A pulse that makes the red dot stay in motion for less time than the original experiment.
Action(s):_____

A pulse that makes the red dot travel a further distance than in the original experiment.
Action(s):_____

(a) move hand more quickly (but still only up and down once and still by the same amount)

(b) move hand more slowly (but still only up and down once and still by the same amount)

(c) move hand a larger distance but up and down in the same amount of time

(d) move hand a smaller distance but up and down in the same amount of time

(e) use a heavier string of the same length, under the same tension

(f) use a lighter string of the same length, under the same tension

(g) use a sting of the same density, but decrease the tension

(h) use a sting of the same density, but increase the tension

(i) put more force into the wave

(j) put less force into the wave

(k) none of the above

---

[21] For research associated with this question see Wittmann, M. C., Steinberg, R. N., & Redish, E. F. (1999). Making sense of how students make sense of mechanical waves. *Phys. Teach., 37.*

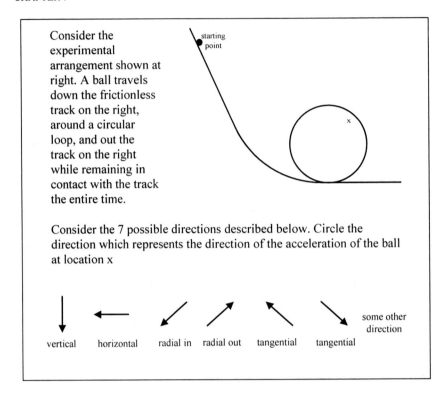

Consider the experimental arrangement shown at right. A ball travels down the frictionless track on the right, around a circular loop, and out the track on the right while remaining in contact with the track the entire time.

Consider the 7 possible directions described below. Circle the direction which represents the direction of the acceleration of the ball at location x

| vertical | horizontal | radial in | radial out | tangential | tangential | some other direction |

ALBERT EINSTEIN

It is safe to say that no one would question the greatness of Einstein as a scientist or his love of science. Like every physicist I know, I have always marveled at his brilliance. When he speaks science, all should listen. His first quote at the beginning of this chapter warns us of the danger of perverting the very beauty of science. His second quote warns us of the danger of prioritizing that which is easiest to test over that which is most important to learn. I know that I am listening.

THE TWO FACES OF AARON

Race, culture, and community

The function of education is to teach one to think intensively and to think critically. Intelligence plus character - that is the goal of true education.

- Martin Luther King

FEBRUARY 26: WAS THAT THE SAME KID?

I am white, Jewish, and Ivy League educated. The great majority (probably the entirety) of my students came from families where no one had any of these characteristics. I might have felt completely at ease doing my thing to the best of my ability, but I was a foreigner to the students. In this school, being new and being a foreigner were 2 strikes against me.

Mr. Jackson was a veteran teacher at UHS whom I admired greatly. He was a Black man who clearly came across as strong and caring. He was recognized as a successful teacher by the staff and students. I was fortunate that Mr. Jackson was willing to help out a new teacher like me. He asked about how things were going and listened to what I had to say. He offered sensible advice and I was happy to listen. He also invited me to visit his class.

I observed Mr. Jackson one day in late February ready to learn. His class was motivating and inspiring. His ability to connect his students to the material being covered was outstanding. However, I don't think that many of his strategies could have been replicated by me. During the day of my observation of him, he made references to "Church on Sunday," to what "your momma and dad" want, and to how his students don't have "a rich uncle that will leave them anything."

Aaron was in Mr. Jackson's class. He was also in one of my classes. In my class, Aaron was sour and non-participatory. He requested to go to the bathroom as often as permitted (actually more). When he was in the classroom he often just put his head on his desk and closed his eyes. His few substantive contributions in my class suggested that he was bright, but they were few and far between no matter what I tried. For Mr. Jackson, Aaron was sitting front and center smiling and participating intelligently. I wish I were able to elicit the same kind of Aaron that Mr. Jackson did. I wish Aaron would have given me a chance before dropping my class.

It wasn't only teachers who looked like the students who were able to connect to the kids the way Mr. Jackson did, but it was relevant. Regardless, for inquiry learning to work, students must be engaged. In getting students engaged, race, culture, and community matter.

WHAT DID HE SAY?

Mr. Hernandez was another veteran teacher at UHS. He was definitely not a foreigner to the kids. He was also enormously respected by students, teachers, administrators, parents, and certainly by me. He cared about the kids. He knew the school system and the community. He was firm and assertive.[1] Even though he knew the rules teachers were supposed to follow, he did what he wanted, and everyone appreciated it.

Like Mr. Jackson (and so many other outstanding teacher leaders that I encountered) Mr. Hernandez was generous with his support to new teachers. This included me. There was many a time when I had a problem with classroom management, particular kids, or unwieldy circumstances that I went to him. Never mind me learning by inquiry, when Mr. Hernandez talked, I just listened.

One day I was walking the halls during a free period with Mr., Hernandez, once again picking his brains. We encountered several students socializing in the stairwell when they were supposed to be in class. He singled out one young Black girl that he knew. (He knew everyone.) She had no excuse for being there. Sarcastically he said to her "Ten years from now it will be White man's fault."

His meaning was clear to her and to me. Here was a young woman given every opportunity to succeed and she was electing to not capitalize on it. Success in this high school was a ticket to a future of her choice, but she was not engaging to the satisfaction of Mr. Hernandez. He talked and she listened, at least in the moment. She apologized and went straight to class.

MR. SMITH AND MR. JONES

Mr. Smith and Mr. Jones were two teachers that I had the chance to observe in class and speak with out of class. Neither was originally from New York City. Both went into education wanting to be good teachers. Both were frustrated about the realities of teaching in their respective schools.[2] Both blamed the students. Mr. Smith was white. Mr. Jones was black.

Mr. Smith was truly outstanding in his understanding of the subject matter but was very inexperienced as a teacher. His class was chaos. He screamed just to get over the volume of the kids. Things were flying. Students roamed about the room during the lesson. It was sad for me to watch.

Mr. Smith might have been out of touch with what content students were able to understand and not understand. The students might have found him boring, despite his obvious passion for the subject he was teaching. His handwriting was pretty poor. His accent made it hard for some students to follow. But he did not deserve to be treated the way he was by his students. There was no excuse for them to have been doing the things that they were doing.

---

[1] I once asked a student to take off his hat during a fire drill without success. Mr. Hernandez went up to the student, took off his hat, and smacked him in the head. The conversation was over.

[2] The demographics in each of their schools were similar to UHS.

I felt nothing but sorrow when Mr. Smith stated to me outside of the classroom:

I look into their eyes and know there is something organically wrong with these kids. The only reason I do not take out a gun and shoot them is because I would go to prison.

How could anyone treat a teacher the way he was treated? How can any teacher think these things about children?

Mr. Jones was less impressive with his understanding of the content. He was a long time tenured New York City public school teacher. His classes had all the characteristics of traditional science lessons. I found them uninspiring. While his style was not a model in terms of classroom management, there were far fewer behavioral problems than there were in Mr. Smith's class.

Mr. Jones had the reputation of being ineffective as an educator and not particularly liked by the students. However, he knew the rituals of control that students were used to. With frustration, he executed them. Regardless, I again felt nothing but sorrow when Mr. Jones shared with me:

This is not a school. It is a jungle to keep these kids off the streets.

How can someone who wanted to be a teacher think like this? And if he did, why did he keep teaching for so long?[3]

There were a lot of teachers who shared opinions like those of Mr. Smith and Mr. Jones. There were a lot of reasons for those opinions.

ANTONIO AND KEISHA

The context in which the students lived mattered. I learned this repeatedly from many of my students, including Antonio and Keisha.[4] They were representative of many students.

Antonio was a young man in my class from the local community. He was a weak student who was frequently a distraction in class. It was clear though that calls home from a teacher were a huge nuisance for him, so he did not usually push it too far. Like so many of my students, he came from a troubled background. I learned details of this background inadvertently one day while I was teaching.

During one lesson, Antonio was socializing with his neighbor without so much as the courtesy to whisper. I asked Antonio politely to stop talking. He looked at

---

[3] It is a flawed system that enables Mr. Jones to maintain his position as a public school teacher through his disdain for his students and through his incompetence as an educator. It is noteworthy though that his ability to maintain order in the classroom and get students to succeed at a reasonable rate on the Regents were *not* the measures which were revealing of his incompetence.

[4] Antonio and Keisha are completely fictional, but they represent composite representations of real students and real events.

me, paused, turned back to his neighbor and continued as if I had said nothing. This same sequence repeated a second and third time with the same outcome.

I took out the appropriate form required to send Antonio to the "resource room." Apparently Antonio did not like that. Let's just say that his reaction was loud and aggressive. (It turns out that based on Antonio's personal history that I had every reason to feel intimidated.) Unsure of what to do, I just kept writing. Actually, I ran out of things to write but I continued with a writing motion anyway. Luckily this turned out to be a good strategy as Antonio's friends used my continued "writing" as a reason to convince him to stop ranting and just go to the resource room before he got into even more trouble. Good thing no one looked at the form that I had in front of me as it was mostly blank.

This incident was meaningful enough that I followed up with the guidance counselor. Ms. Rosen was caring, competent, and idealistic, but after 20 years at UHS she was also pragmatic and weathered. After telling Ms. Rosen that it was Antonio, she took out his file. The thickness of the file was my first clue that there were issues. The newspaper clipping on the top was my second clue. Six months earlier, Antonio's mother had been killed in front of Antonio in gang related violence. All of a sudden, socializing in class seemed like a ridiculous thing to be talking about.

Keisha was a young woman in a different class than Antonio. She was bright and occasionally did solid work, but more often did very poorly. She never seemed happy in class, but never left me with the feeling that it had anything to do with me or with physics.

It was obvious that Keisha was struggling with issues beyond which I was able to appreciate. She routinely walked into class late, eating food, and drinking soda. All of this was violation of school rules. Each time I confronted Keisha with the rules and consequences. Each time Keisha snapped at me angrily. "Alright already, leave me alone." "You said that yesterday." "Go call my mother, I don't care." Each time there was an extended interruption to the class.

The repeated pattern of this behavior resulted in the mandated protocol of escalating consequences. A drink of soda in class resulted in another phone call home which apparently did not go well for Keisha. Later that same day, I learned that Keisha was pregnant. I realized quickly how little drinking soda in class mattered.

MORE FROM MR. HERNANDEZ

One day a student that I did not know walked into my class in the middle of a lesson. He wandered around the room, chatted with the students in the class, went to the front of the room as if to assume the role of the teacher, and went through my personal belongings in the teacher's closet. All this was to the amusement of the rest of the class. He would not leave when I asked him to. He would not identify himself. He was gone before the Dean arrived.

With the help of Mr. Hernandez, I found out that the student was Lavernius. Like Garry, Lavernius was a routine offender of school rules (and the law). He was in perpetual trouble, but was somehow without risk of being removed from the school. Naturally I followed Mr. Hernandez's advice on how to proceed. He arranged for Lavernius to come apologize to me directly. I am not sure what Lavernius would do if anyone else had told him to, but this was Mr. Hernandez so he obliged.

When Lavernius met with me there was no denial. There was no contrition. There was barely an apology. It was clear that there would have been no apology at all if Mr. Hernandez were not sitting next to me. Lavernius's explanation for interrupting my class was that his regular teacher was absent that day and the door to my classroom was open. He seemed to think that this was a legitimate justification for his behavior.

After the meeting I asked Mr. Hernandez what he thought. He told me that I should accept Lavernius's apology, weak as it was, and move on. I trusted him and followed his advice, but thought that this seemed like a mild consequence. He agreed, but told me that Lavernius's actions were a result of the way you learn to treat people "growing up in the projects." Calling his parents or any of the other realistic options would not help. They would only escalate the situation.

Of course I followed Mr. Hernandez's advice. I told him though that if Lavernius had done this out of school that I would have called the police. He told me that if this had happened out of school, I would have been dead.

AND MORE FROM MR. HERNANDEZ

Poor Mr. Hernandez would have to hear from me every time I got frustrated. It was his own fault. He always knew what to say.

One day I wrote in my journal the following:

I spoke with Mr. Hernandez again today. I told him how hard it is to get some of the kids to succeed even at a small level. He said I should do a simple homework with (for?) them in class and then give practically the same problem on the test. I said this did not feel like teaching and he agreed, but he said that is the way it needs to be for many of them. I believe him. He is bright and understands the kids and their real needs.

A second journal entry from later that same day contrasted with Mr. Hernandez's recommendation:

In our professional development workshop today we talked about the importance of working our way up Bloom's taxonomy. 'Regurgitating' information is not good enough. This is a very interesting juxtaposition with Mr. Hernandez's comments a few hours ago.

A juxtaposition that I struggled with all year.

REFLECTIONS ON RACE, CULTURE, AND COMMUNITY

The relationship between race, culture, community, and school education at UHS is way bigger than I could learn in a year. It is much more that I could write about in a chapter. An overwhelming year though left me with some opinions, particularly related to my perspectives on science education. To teach by and about inquiry the students need to be engaged. For the students to be engaged, the teacher needs to be able to make connections to the students and to the contexts of their lives. I needed to do a better job at this to achieve the goals that I wanted to achieve.

There is more though. I might not have understood the students as well as I wanted, but I was trying. I was trying really hard. So was Mr. Smith. So were many other frustrated teachers. I imagine that some time long ago, so was Mr. Jones. There needs to be accountability by the students. They need to give us a chance. We can't all be as good as Mr. Jackson, or Mr. Hernandez, or Ms. O'Brien, but we have a lot to offer.

STRATEGIES THAT WORK: MAKING CONNECTIONS

Many strategies needed to address the challenges described in this chapter transcend teaching science by inquiry. How can Mr. Smith be put in a position to succeed? Should Mr. Jones be out of a job? How can high achieving graduates of the community be incented to teach in the community in which they grew up? How can schools, parents, students, and communities work together on solutions? In the next chapter I go into some of what I learned at UHS and how optimistic I am that success could be achieved.

With respect to my goal of teaching science by inquiry, I looked back at the assignments that I gave and it is remarkable how the majority of them are far from the real lives that my students had. It did not have to be that way though, certainly not all of the time. There were many opportunities to learn about science right in the context in which the students lived, especially since they lived in New York City.

Below are two activities which are designed to connect what was in my students' backyard to the content, skills, and dispositions that I was trying to teach. The first is a simple activity on kinematic variables that can be conducted on the subway. The second is a student engineered assignment that takes advantage of the informal learning environments ubiquitous throughout the city. Students have ample opportunity to focus on a topics of importance, interest, and relevance to them.

Homework on the way home

In answering the following questions, consider at least two subway stops apart on any route that you take.

1. Use a map and a watch with a second hand to estimate the average velocity of the train. Explain how you determined the answer.

2. Time how long the train traveled near peak speed. Explain how you know how to time this.

3. Estimate the maximum speed of the train. Explain your reasoning.

4. Draw a rough graph of the entire subway ride. Label your axes clearly.

5. Explain quantitatively how your graph is consistent with your answers to 1. through 3. above.

Museum visit assignment

To answer the following questions, choose an exhibit at the New York Hall of Science, the Museum of Natural History, or the Liberty Science Center that you find interesting and connects to some topic covered in class.

1. Describe your choice of exhibit and how it connects to class. Include a detailed sketch and summary of the exhibit.

2. Answer any 2 of the following 4 items in detail:

   a. Describe the big idea that is that is being demonstrated. How is that big idea being shown?

   b. Name one observation that you made. Name something that can be inferred from that observation.

   c. Relate specifically some aspect of the exhibit to an equation, graph, or diagram that we covered in class.

   d. Make a connection between a physical principal being demonstrated in the exhibit and an application that you encounter in your everyday life.

MARTIN LUTHER KING

Who better to look to for words of wisdom on race, culture, community, and education than Martin Luther King? He routinely spoke words that moved masses. In his quote at the beginning of this chapter, he points to the need to build and connect education, intensive thinking, and character. Teachers and students alike need to heed his words.

STUDENTS CREATE A REFERENCE TABLE

Systems thinking

Classrooms aren't supposed to be mindless automatons. They are supposed to produce them.

- Stephen Colbert

MARCH 10: A DIFFERENT KIND OF REFERENCE TABLE

As winter turned to spring, my period 7 class was still the one that went most smoothly. It was far from perfect, but all year I felt like I made a better overall connection with this class. This connection translated into fewer classroom management problems, more dialogue, better instruction and more learning.

I wish that I understood what was happening in Period 7 well enough to have replicated it in my other classes. I didn't. I wish that I now had a well defined prescription to share with new science teachers that I work with at CCNY. I don't. I wish that I had confidence that with more experience I would be able to improve my ability to succeed as a teacher. I do!

My positive relationship with the class fed on itself. When things went well, I was more myself and more effective as a teacher. As I was more myself and more effective as a teacher, things went well. Unfortunately the opposite snowball effect happened in my other classes.

For my period 7 class, I had the relationship where they taught me the language of the kids in the school. It wasn't much, but they greeted me with a "What's crackin'?" when they walked into class and I shot back a "What's poppin'?"

One period 7 student interrupted me with an oddly spoken "Pause!" during class. I asked what that meant. She eagerly told me. After a few other similar exchanges it got to the point where during some free time a group of students produced a reference table for my use. Figure 9.1 shows part of the table. They called it "Steinberg's reference table." When they said something to me that I did not understand, I stopped class and looked it up deliberately. If it was not on my reference table, I added it at the end. Every so often I used one of the expressions in the flow of the class to the obvious approval of the students. If I completely botched the usage they were particularly delighted.

CHAPTER 9

It would be wrong to say that period 7 classroom esprit was better *because* I made a connection with the students. It would be wrong to say that I was able to make a connection with the students in period 7 *because* there was better esprit. It went both ways, and it was entangled with the personalities of the kids in the class, the time of day, my having already gone through two other sections with similar lesson plans that day, and so much more. Many things were interconnected as a complex system. Regardless, one way or another, connecting with the students was connected to class going better.

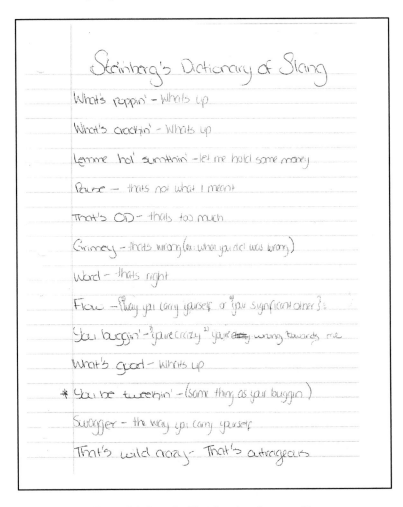

Figure 9.1. Page 1 of Steinberg's reference table.

MIGUEL AND JORGE

Miguel was a very bright and articulate student in my senior level elective class. However, most of the time he was class clown, always pushing the envelope with his explicit language and sexual references. It did not matter that what was in his head had nothing to do with what was happening in class. He blurted it out anyway, at any time. He was rebellious and not at all concerned about what teachers thought of him. Or so it seemed.

Somehow Miguel and I had a very positive relationship. I think it was because I was hard on him, but with more than a touch of humor. I think his reward for me was that he would engage in challenging material, at least once in a while when he felt like it. When he did I was impressed, and I told him so.

On Miguel's report card, alongside a mediocre grade, I put the teacher comment *"Special aptitude in this field."* (I also put *"Has ability to do better."*) He came to class the next day beaming "You think I'm smart," noting what I put on his report card. I told Miguel that I only put that comment in because there was no *"Pain in the ass"* box for me to check. I think he liked that comment even more.

If I had a different set of expectations for Miguel our relationship could have been a disaster. But we got along well and I think Miguel got some reasonable value out of the class. I still think Miguel had real aptitude. I still think Miguel was a pain in the ass.

Jorge was in Miguel's class. He was mostly quiet and pleasant, but made zero attempts to do any of the school work. I would try to integrate him into the flow of the class both during group work and whole class discussions. With a smile, Jorge would respectfully evade my attempts to engage him. He would apologize for not knowing something, throw out some meaningless collection of technical words, or change the subject. I think he would have done anything to just get me to move on to someone else. I also tried to engage Jorge on a more social level during free time. His disposition was similar.

One marking period Jorge explained that it was really important to pass so that he could play ball. There was no way that he had earned a passing grade. Shockingly (to him and to me) I told Jorge that I would pass him anyway. This was totally against my policy and personality. It was not something I did any other time before or since, but I wanted to follow my gut and see if I could make a difference with Jorge.

I told him that I would pass him that one time and that I would not ask for any promises or other conditions. I just asked that he make an honest effort to do well going forward. Jorge said that he would. He thanked me and I passed him. For the rest of the school year, there was not a single improvement in Jorge's performance or approach. I might not have been successful this time, but I never stopped trying to do what it takes.

PERIOD 9

Some of my best feelings about being a teacher came from when I was with the kids outside of normal school hours. After one "period 9" [1] extra-help session I wrote the following in my journal:

> *Students were at extra-help being themselves today and I was being myself. I loved it. We were having fun. They wanted to do and understand physics and I had that feeling about why I love being a teacher.*

> *Carlos opened up to me some. He wants to be an engineer. He is an outstanding student, but does not try at all. He followed me as I was leaving and continued to talk. I advised him on some extra-curricular possibilities and he listened excitedly.*

> *Linda (who never comes to class) showed up and did the make-up lab with transparent tape. She is so far from passing that there is no grade benefit to her, but she did the whole thing anyway and said "This is fun."*

Another example of after school success was a result of the coincidence that several of my students were on the basketball team. I was able to travel and attend one of their road games. That night, I wrote in my journal:

> *My time at the game was among the most fun as a teacher ever. When I got there, my students were visibly happy to see me. Latrell asked for extra credit for each point he scored. I asked if he should lose credit for each turnover. Three students NOT in my class ran to me and asked me lots of questions about Einstein's Theory of Relativity.*

> *I had to leave before the game was over. Joseph (who was not normally particularly friendly) shouted from on the court "Where are you going Mr. Steinberg?" It was very sweet.*

My next sabbatical I'm going to do that more often. [2]

PARENT-TEACHER NIGHT

Parent-teacher night brought out every kind of interaction that I could have imagined. Most parents were respectful and appreciative, asking questions about their children and the class. Their dispositions ran the gamut. Some promised

---

[1] Period 9 was after the normal school day when I would be available in my classroom to students for any reason.

[2] Addendum from wife: the next sabbatical is going to be on a beach in Greece.

better behavior, performance, or effort from their children. Some were hostile, frankly out of touch with what their children were like in school.

In addition to learning about the parents, Parent-teacher night was also a great way to learn about students such as Joan and Pedro. Both of these students had parents share with me positive comments their children told them about being in my class.

Joan's mother said her daughter liked my class very much. I saw Joan as quiet. Only after some reflection was I not surprised about her mother's comment. Joan did not volunteer much during class time, but her written work indicated that she was intelligently processing what was being covered, and apparently with enough enthusiasm to share with her mother.

Pedro had the appearance and reputation that suggested that he would never want to take a class like physics. He was a rough athlete who sported gang colors outside of school. However his mother said physics was one of his favorite classes. Awkwardly I noted to her that her son had not submitted the most recent homework. Pedro, who happened to be with her, said it was in his locker and he did not turn it in because it was late.

This sure sounded like a story to me so I called his bluff. I told him that if he got it and turned it in I would give him full credit. To my surprise, he eagerly got up, retrieved his homework from his locker, and turned it in on the spot. The work was thoughtful and well done. I happily gave him the credit.

Neither Joan nor Pedro followed through with their courses the way I was hoping, but at least I saw a window into some success and opportunity. I never would have known but for parent-teacher night.

PROJECT BASED LEARNING

In all my work with high school science teachers, Mr. Diaz was the most impressive educator that I have encountered. He taught biology concepts through having his students do extended projects. All over his classroom, things were growing, swimming, rotting, and stinking. Yes, I found this to be a good thing.[3]

Students had the opportunity to pick the topic of the project, with Mr. Diaz's guidance to ensure that the project was relevant and fruitful. Whether they picked about plants, food, or fish, it was projects that they had a say in.

Mr. Diaz then coached each student brilliantly through every step of the way including choosing a research question, researching background material, setting up the experiment, collecting data, analyzing results, writing a report, and giving a presentation to the class. He was amazing at getting students excited about a topic that was meaningful to them and helpful at learning critical concepts about the subject matter of the course. On top of that, students were doing real science. I wish I had Mr. Diaz's skill as a science teacher.

---

[3] I found things growing, swimming, rotting, and stinking in other classrooms too, but since those were not biology classes I did not find that to be a good thing.

I asked Mr. Diaz how he was able to balance doing such interesting work with preparing students for the Regents exam. He said it was not easy. It's a pity that his teaching the way he did was in conflict with preparing students for the state test. It's an even bigger pity that a teacher who wants to teach the way that Mr. Diaz did has a disincentive to being a teacher.

DELAYED REACTION

Janet was a senior and only needed a half credit of science to graduate, so she was only in my elective physics class for the first half of the year. She was argumentative and disruptive. My first encounter with her was an extended exchange about her using a cell phone in class on the first day of school. The result was a visit from the Dean. But Janet was also extremely bright, having as much reasoning skill as anyone in any of my classes.

Janet participated when she was so moved. When she did, her contributions were outstanding. I tried to challenge her, but she did not seem that interested. Regardless, I would not let the opportunity to engage meaningfully with someone as smart as Janet slip through my fingers, so I kept trying. Sometimes it worked. Sometimes it didn't.

After doing her time for her needed half credit, I did not see Janet for a while after she left my class in January. Then one day in March we crossed paths in the hallway. Janet smiled and shouted out warmly "Mr. Steinberg!" She came up to me and gave me a hug. She offered positive feedback for having been in my class. It made me feel that I reached her at least somewhat and that she appreciated it. As a teacher who cares, I appreciated that.

Better late than never.

BACK TO ANTONIO AND KEISHA

Soon after my encounter with Antonio from last chapter, there was a long weekend. Class ended early the last day of school before the break and I went over and talked with him. "What do you do when you're not in school?" "Where do you see yourself in five years?" Despite all of my challenges adjusting to UHS, I really think most of the students saw me as friendly, accessible, and caring, so I usually got a pretty good conversation going on days like those.

Antonio said the predictable "You don't get what it's like" and such. (I hear that from my own children too.) We went back and forth playfully. Then he said "Not everyone is like you. Some people just bag groceries, go home and do what they do." He described some of the respectable activities that interest him and gave me a realistic outlook of where he was going after high school. Understanding concepts of physics was not part of it, and that was clear to him.

I told Antonio that I respected what he had to say, but I hoped that he could find a way to get value out of class anyway. He just smiled. Antonio and I got along well the rest of the year. There was not a lot of physics learning, but I hope that a few of the general skills that I was trying to teach got through. I know that he taught me.

That same day before the long weekend, I tried to talk with Keisha. She wanted nothing to do with me and the conversation went nowhere. She engaged little with me or my class the rest of the year. I did not know what to do.

REFLECTIONS ON SYSTEMS THINKING

Garry, Marlon, Aaron, and Jorge highlighted my failings as a teacher at UHS. Ms. O'Brien, Mr. Jackson, Mr. Hernandez, and Mr. Diaz all taught me that it is possible to succeed if you know how to connect to the students. Miguel, Carlos, Linda, Joan, Pedro, Janet, and my period 7 class gave me hope that I can connect too.

My goals included great gains in student ability to think, reason, and understand physics. My knowing the material and how to teach it was not enough. Antonio and Keisha reminded me that my capacity to succeed is intimately connected to whether my students are ready and able to learn. Trauma in students' personal lives matters. Lack of a home support system matters. What students eat matters. So much more matters.

Children, their schools, teachers, families, and communities are complex systems with many interdependent dimensions. What happens outside of class impacts what happens inside of class. What happens at school affects what happens at home. What happens at home changes the way students interact with their teachers. And so on.

Expecting schooling to be successful by just thinking about classroom lessons is like expecting to understand science by memorizing the reference table. Affectively, socially, physiologically, and even cognitively we need to recognize the many facets of each student's life. We need to start with recognition of the way students and the worlds around them really are.

STRATEGIES THAT WORK: MAKING MORE CONNECTIONS

Students and teachers at UHS taught me how to make connections to them about what matters to them outside the boundaries of curriculum and instruction. With respect to class activities, many of the strategies that work regarding making connections to students have been discussed already. Students being able to achieve real understanding of the material is a good start. Having assignments that students enjoy is always a good idea. When assignment topics are tied to the students' lives and communities it is even better. Mr. Diaz taught me how to connect by having students take more control of the learning environment and activities, under his guidance of course.

Below I outline two assignments which are intended to help bridge the material learned in class to what matters to the students. Each could be an extensive culminating project done near the end of the year or a much smaller assignment integrated with the content coverage of a given week. As with Mr. Diaz's projects, continuous consultation with the teacher is expected. All student work need be of the appropriate depth, scope, and subject matter.

For the student designed project, students use an exploration into something of interest to them to develop their understanding of the content covered in class. Examples of activities range from javelin toss to roller coasters to cooking. Examples of devices range from Wii to GPS to cameras. For the student report, students select something from current events that they find interesting. It could be as wide reaching as global warming or as specific as a crime scene investigation.

Student designed projects

Select a science related activity or device which connects a real world interest of yours to a physics principle studied in class.

1. Describe your activity or device in your own words.

2. Describe the related physics principle studied in class.

3. Describe in detail how your description in 2. is related to your description in 1. How does the physics principle account for the implementation of your activity or functioning of your device? Explain.

4. Based on what you have learned about physics, speculate on what modification of your activity or device can result in an improvement (in performance or scope of use) that you find interesting.

Student report

Select a science related item in the news which you find interesting. Write a report about how scientific content and reasoning is related to the news item.

STEVEN COLBERT

Stephen Colbert might be the least impressive sage cited in this book and his quote about automatons was part of a commentary about robots in Japan. But this (sarcastic?) comment resonated with me and my experience at UHS. To be successful as a teacher we can not treat all classes and students the same. And as he suggests,[4] it cuts both ways. We do not want to graduate students who lack the capacity for independent thoughts and ideas.

---

[4] At least I think I know what he is suggesting. I am never sure with him.

IGNORE WHAT YOU LEARNED IN CLASS

Connecting school learning with the real world

A child of five would understand this. Send someone to fetch a child of five.

- Groucho Marx

APRIL 25: THE TWO VERSION WORKSHEET EXPERIMENT

It was late in the year and I was trying to balance getting students ready for the Regents with getting my students to learn and approach physics like a scientist. I was not satisfied with how well I was doing either, but I never stopped trying.

All year I tried to get students to make sense of what they were doing and not just plow through equations and terminology. I wanted to teach them that this kind of sense making of the material could even improve their grade on the Regents. I went through examples of how connecting motion questions to what they already knew about how things moved was helpful. I made explicit how relating force problems to what they saw happen in the real world was a great way to get started. I showed them how making reasonable estimates of temperature in calorimetry calculations was an easy way to check your work. As a science teacher I think that strategies such as these can be practiced and developed in class. They can then be transferred to other domains. What a wonderful opportunity!

As the year progressed though, I did not feel like I was achieving my goal of connecting class work to my students' life experiences. In response, I came up with an idea to see just how much students were making connections and to work towards helping them do so.

I gave all of my classes an independent in-class worksheet with 10 questions in the domain of physics. Each of the questions on the worksheet could be answered without relying on the formalism from class or on the reference tables. For example, a truck starting from rest accelerates at a rate of 5 miles per hour each second for 4 seconds. What is the final velocity of the truck? This question can be answered with the tools of the physics curricula (with the equations of motion) or by thinking about a truck speeding up by 5 mph four times. All 10 worksheet questions with solutions and comments are given at the end of this chapter.

I decided to put a little twist on it though when I administered the worksheet. I created 2 versions. The questions were identical in both versions, but the instructions were different. One set of instructions used language from the Regents exam:

Version 1: *"Use your reference tables to answer the following questions. Show all work including the equation and substitution with units."*

The other set of instructions read:

Version 2: *"In answering the following questions, do NOT use your reference tables. Answer the questions how you would have answered them had you never taken a physics class. Explain how you determined your answers."*

Students with version 1 were given the reference table. Students with version 2 were not.

Quantitative details of the results are hard to interpret. One reason is that I made no attempt to systematically select which students completed which version. Another reason is that it was late in the year and more than a few students put their heads on their desks for the entire time, seemingly without regard to my little experiment.

Nevertheless, I did see some clear, alarming trends. The average score on version 1 was 46%. The average score on version 2 was 58%.[1] After spending well over 100 hours with my students, they performed better on solving problems when I told them to pretend they never knew me. This was a blow to my already diminished ego.

The success rate was higher for the students who were asked to pretend they never had physics. In addition, these students often went about the problem more sensibly than students who were asked to use their reference tables. Figures 10.1 and 10.2 show two representative responses for the question about the truck speeding up. Figures 10.3 and 10.4 show two representative responses for a question where students were told the wavelength of a wave and then asked what the wavelength was.

In each of these two examples, the student who attempted to do what was taught in class and use what was written on the reference table made no sense. In each of these two examples, the student who pretended to have never taken physics executed the problem sensibly and successfully.

When I went over the worksheet in class, I confessed to all the students what I had done and why. I shared the contrast in student performance with the two different sets of instructions. I explained the value of making connections to the real world while going through Regents questions, but they seemed to think that my questions were not like Regents questions. They were "trick" questions. I think that I made my point, but I doubt that I had the impact that I wanted in the way they subsequently approached schooling and testing.

---

[1] The difference in these numbers is certainly not statistically reliable, but their depressing impact is very real.

7. A truck starting from rest accelerates at a rate of 5 miles per hour each second for 4 seconds. What is the final velocity of the truck?

$$U_F = 3$$

$$U_F = U_i + at$$

$$U_i = 5m^s$$

$$U_F = 5m/s + (9.8 m/s^2)(4 sec)$$

$$a = 9.8 m/s^2$$

$$U_F = 5m/s + 39.9 m/s$$

$$t = 4 sec$$

$$U_F = 44.2 m/s$$

Figure 10.1. Sample student response to accelerating truck question for student instructed to use reference table. Student confused units and used acceleration due to gravity value from reference table (which is irrelevant to problem) in coming up with incorrect answer.

7. A truck starting from rest accelerates at a rate of 5 miles per hour each second for 4 seconds. What is the final velocity of the truck?

For each second it would add 5 and my answer would be 20

Figure 10.2. Sample student response to accelerating truck question for student instructed to pretend to have never taken physics. Student demonstrated conceptual understanding of acceleration and came up with correct answer sensibly.

9. Consider a wave with wavelength 2.5cm and frequency 40Hz. What is the wavelength of the wave?

$$v = f \lambda$$

$$\frac{v}{f} = \lambda$$

$$\frac{v}{40Hz} = \lambda$$

$$10 c^s \lambda$$

Figure 10.3. Sample student response to wavelength question for student instructed to use reference table. Student futilely attempted to use relevant looking formula from reference table.

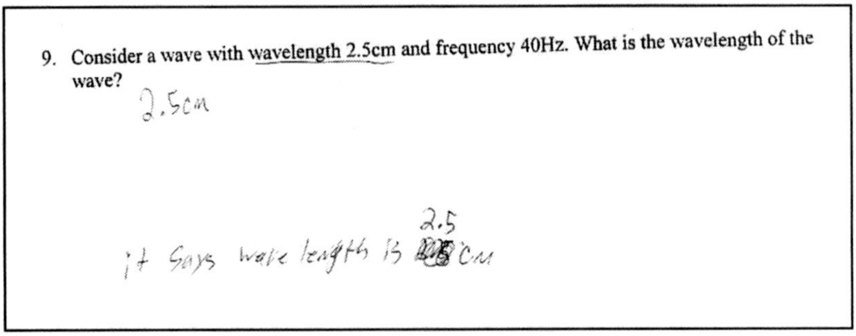

Figure 10.4. Sample student response to wavelength question for student instructed to pretend to have never taken physics. Student answered simple question simply.

I DIDN'T SEE THAT COMING

I anticipated that seeing the instructions on version 2 would get students to recognize that these are questions that could be answered by just thinking about what was being asked. I noted in my journal how one student therefore caught me off guard:

> *Isaac handed in a mostly blank worksheet and told me "I do not know how to do this without the reference tables."*

That was not the mindset I was hoping for.

OTHER VERSIONS OF THE TWO VERSION EXPERIMENT WITH ONLY ONE VERSION

I tailored the specific questions on my worksheet to my context and objectives at UHS. However, I was in part inspired by my previous implementations of the "Force Concept Inventory" (FCI).[2]

The FCI is a 29 multiple-choice question diagnostic in introductory mechanics developed by David Hestenes and colleagues. The questions are asked more in common language instead of the language of classroom physics problems. For example, one question asks about the flight of a golf ball. Another asks what happens when the cable holding an elevator car breaks.

I have administered the FCI dozens of times to thousands of students. Results have been overwhelmingly clear and consistent with the results of hundreds of thousands of other students who have taken this diagnostic. Student success on the FCI is lower than physics instructors expect or hope for. In classes where instruction is largely traditional, student improvement on the FCI is extremely

---

[2]   Hestenes, D. Wells, M. and Swackhammer, G. "Force concept inventory," *Phys. Teach.*, **30**, (1992).

small. In classes where instruction includes active student engagement, student improvement on the FCI is better. The consistency of these results across levels, institutions, and eras is impressive. Contexts range from high school through Harvard University.[3]

There are conceptual tests similar to the FCI in many other areas.[4] Each yield similar results. Students say and write things which surprise and disappoint their instructors. Traditional instruction does not seem to help. Gains can be achieved when students are engaged and attention is paid to how they learn, but these gains are often modest.

However, as far as I know there have been no attempts to ask students to ignore what they learned in any implementation of any of these diagnostics. I am thinking now though that maybe this should be tried more often.

"OKAY, BUT I STILL DON'T BELIEVE IN EVOLUTION"

Unfortunately, there are many areas in science where students do not see reality and class work as connected. Several of my students at CCNY, all practicing high school biology teachers, have done research projects on student understanding of evolution. Their results are worrisome. Their students do not "believe" in evolution, but are willing to write on exams what they know the teacher wants to see.

After instruction, in one of the most important and compelling scientific theories that there is, students are either unable or unwilling to believe the results. They are however willing to put whatever the teacher wants on the exam.

REFLECTIONS ON MAKING CONNECTIONS TO THE REAL WORLD

What does it say about what we are doing if students succeed more at answering questions about what we are teaching them when they ignore what we have taught them? Or that they do not believe what they are "learning" but humor the teacher in the classroom anyway? I want to work towards teaching my students how to think, reason, and succeed in the real world. If students do not see any reason to connect what we are teaching to the way they think outside of the classroom, then we have to question the value of what we are doing. If students see what they are learning as unrelated to what happens outside of school, then we have to adjust the way we make connections to the real world when we teach. It seems once again though that telling students outright what to do and think is not having the impact that we want.

---

[3] I was amused once at a conference presentation by Prof. Eric Mazur of Harvard University when he described his introduction to the FCI. He confessed how he was skeptical that his students would have any difficulty with the FCI ("not Harvard students"). He eagerly administered it to one of his classes. He then shared how shocking it was when one of his students immediately raised her hand to ask "How do you want me to answer these questions, by how you taught us or according to how we really think?"

[4] See the end of chapter 7 for a list of references.

STRATEGIES THAT WORK: MAKING EVEN MORE CONNECTIONS

Making connections consistently emerges as a priority in effective teaching strategies, both in my teaching experiences and in learning theory.[5] There needs to be connections to what students already know, to students' real lives and interests, to related contexts, and to the real world.

Below are two more examples of science problems where students need to make connections. For the first, students need to connect what they are learning in class about conservation of momentum to a simple analysis of a collision between two cars. In addition to seeing that what they are learning in class has real world applications, they need to come up with a problem solving strategy and decide what additional information they need to come up with.

In the second problem, students confront what on the surface is a conflict between what they are learning in class and common sense. Students are not asked to reject blindly what they believed coming into (and will likely believe going out of) class. They are not left with the opportunity to think that class work is different from the real world. Instead, they are given the opportunity to explicitly reconcile how what they are learning in class is in fact consistent with the way they make sense of the real world.

Conservation of momentum and car collisions

A medium sized pickup truck traveling north collides with a compact car traveling east, both on dry pavement. The speed limit for both was 30 mph. The intersection where the collision occurred was at a 4 way stop sign. After the collision, the two cars are stuck together and slide at an angle of 30° clockwise from north. The skid marks start at the location of impact and end 10 meters away where the vehicles come to rest.

In answering the two questions below, support your answers with diagrams and what you have learned about physics. Identify specifically any estimations that you make. Describe your level of confidence in your results.

1. Estimate the ratio of the speeds of the two vehicles when they collided. Explain how you determined your answer.

2. Estimate how fast each vehicle was traveling at the time of impact. Explain how you determined your answer.

Connecting formalism and intuition in the context of Newton's third law

Newton's third law states that if body A exerts a force on body B, then body B exerts an equal and opposite force on body A. However, if a truck moving at a high speed hits a small slow moving car, most people want to say that the

---

[5] For example, see National Research Council, *How people learn: Brain, mind, experience and school*, Washington, DC: National Academic Press (1999).

force on the car is greater than the force on the truck. Explain how the observation of what happens when the truck hits the car is consistent with Newton's third law. Support your explanation with the mathematics of Newton's second law.

GROUCHO MARX

I think that the quote at the beginning of this chapter was intended to be a clever play on words by the great comedian Groucho Marx. I read it now more as tragic comedy, poking fun at how experiences after the traditional age that school starts can hinder the capacity to understand the world.

WORKSHEET SOLUTIONS / COMMENTS

1. Equilibrium exists on an object where three forces are acting on it. If one of the forces is a 7.0N force north and another force is a 3.0N force south, what is the magnitude and direction of the third force?

The 3 forces would have to add to zero so the answer is 4.0N south.

2. On planet X the weight of a 3.0kg rock is 24 pounds. What is the weight of a 6.0kg rock on planet X?

If the mass is doubled, the weight is also doubled, so the answer is 48 pounds.

3. A 0.5 kg ball starts from rest and rolls 2.0 meters down a hill which makes an angle of 45° with respect to the horizontal. (See figure at right.) Is the time it takes the ball to cover the first meter greater than, less than, or equal to the time it takes to cover the second meter?

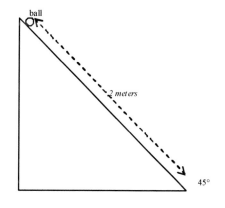

The ball will go slower in the first meter than in the second meter so it will spend more time in the first meter. This can be done quantitatively with Newton's laws and the equations of motion for uniform acceleration as well, but it is much more complicated that way.

4. A wooden block has a mass of 2.5kg and a copper block has a mass of 3.0 kg. Which of the blocks has a greater weight?

Copper: the object with the greater mass has the greater weight, regardless of whether one attempts to use the reference table relationship between the two.

5. The position vs. time graphs for two cars (A and B) are shown at right. Which of the following best describes the velocities of the 2 cars when the 2 lines intersect?
A. *The velocity of car A is greater than the velocity of car B.*
B. *The velocity of car A is less than the velocity of car B.*
C. *The velocity of car A is equal to the velocity of car B.*
D. *There is not enough information to compare the velocities of the two cars.*

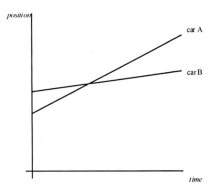

For a position-time graph, a car covering more distance in the same amount of time will have a steeper slope, so the answer is A.

6. The velocity vs. time graphs for two cars (X and Y) are shown at right. Which of the following best describes the velocities of the 2 cars when the 2 lines intersect?
A. *The velocity of car X is greater than the velocity of car Y.*
B. *The velocity of car X is less than the velocity of car Y.*
C. *The velocity of car X is equal to the velocity of car Y.*
D. *There is not enough information to compare the velocities of the two cars.*

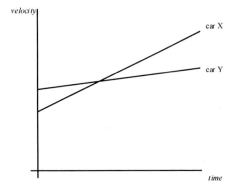

Since at the point that the two lines intersect the velocity readings are the same, the answer is C.

7. A truck starting from rest accelerates at a rate of 5 miles per hour each second for 4 seconds. What is the final velocity of the truck?

The truck starts with velocity zero and then increases it by 5mph four times yielding a final velocity of 20mph. This can be done quantitatively with the equations of motion for uniform acceleration as well but one must be careful with units.

8. When a 20 ounce block hangs from a spring it elongates by 6.0 cm. How much would the spring elongate if a 10 ounce block was hanging from it?

Half the mass will result in half the elongation of 3.0 cm, the answer one would get with the equation of Hooke's law.

9. Consider a wave with wavelength 2.5cm and frequency 40Hz. What is the wavelength of the wave?

The wavelength is given: 2.5 cm. The equation from the reference table that looks relevant relates wavelength, frequency, and wave speed. It is unneeded.

10. A 60cm nichrome wire is used to connect a 15Ω resistor to a battery causing a current of 4 Amperes. If the 60cm nichrome wire is replaced with a 30cm nichrome wire, will the current increase, decrease, or remain the same?

A shorter wire results in less resistance and more current. This can be seen quantitatively with the equation relating resistance and resistivity from the reference table.

PART III

FINISHING AT UHS AND MOVING FORWARD

Making sense of it all

THANK YOU! THANK YOU, SO SMART I AM

Teacher education

Students are then misled into thinking that they have pursued inquiry and possess understanding when they have, in fact, only used technical terms the meaning of which they did not comprehend and only dealt in vacuous generalizations devoid of genuine thought and substance. In such circumstances they are encouraged to embrace the all too widespread rationalization that 'any opinion is just as good as any other opinion.' [1]

- *Arnold Arons*

MAY 28: FULL CIRCLE

By the end of May, my year at UHS was winding down and my transition back to college campus was beginning. I was grateful for the opportunity and support of the principal. I was grateful for all the help of the many wonderful teachers and staff at UHS. I was grateful that I got to know so many wonderful students. With some guilt though, I was also grateful that the year was winding down.

As was usually the case in May, I was reviewing applications for a new group of pre-service middle and high school science teachers. They were coming to City College for an intensive full summer program to prepare to teach in New York City for the first time in September.

As head of the Science Education Program, I get to pick the first activities in which they engage. Every year I pick the *Physics by Inquiry* Astronomy activities from the University of Washington which were used in the Summer Scholars Program. For those first few weeks, we don't talk much about classroom management, Regents exams, or differentiated instruction. Instead, all these soon to be teachers learn science material by inquiry. The material is unknown to most of them.

I watch the teachers reason, justify, and explain. They participate in the process of science as learners. Rather than talking about meaningful science education strategies in the abstract, they recognize and reflect on what it means to learn and know the very material which they are learning.

In the words of Richard Feynman, they also learn "the difference between knowing the name of something and knowing something."

Few of the teachers in the program have any background in astronomy and not one of them is likely to spend a majority of the time teaching it. Remarkably,

---

[1]   Arons, A. *Teaching Introductory Physics* (John Wiley & Sons, NJ, 1997).

the reception to the course is overwhelmingly positive. Academically, the experience and success of the teachers is almost identical to what was described for the participants in the Summer Scholars Program.

More significantly, the teachers boast of a new found perspective of what it means to know and learn science in general. They are excited about becoming science teachers with this emerging perspective.

Not that I want to burst that bubble, but I try to temper this enthusiasm by pointing out the challenges of teaching science in a real urban classroom. From this point on, I think my warnings will come across as more credible and informed as compared to prior to sabbatical. Regardless, while I am certain that there are challenges and frustrations in teaching inquiry science, I am confident that these could be overcome. I trust that both my optimism and caution are conveyed.

TRAFOLINE

It is very important that you learn about trafoline. Trafoline is a new form of zionter. It is montilled in Ceristanna. The Ceritanians gristerlate large amounts of fevan and then bracter it to quasal trafoline. Trafoline may well be one of our most lakized snezlais in the future because of our zionter lescilidge.

TEST:

Directions: Answer the following questions in complete sentences.

1. What is trafoline?

2. Where is trafoline montilled?

3. How is trafoline quasalled?

4. Why is it important to know about trafoline?

Figure 11.1. Classroom handout in science teacher class.

Every summer I distribute a handout with the content shown in Figure 11.1 to the teachers without commenting on it or giving instructions.[2] At first most just read it

---

[2] This trafoline handout was first given to me by Arnold Arons. After using it in class with great success I thanked him for it. I proudly told him how I credited him to my students. He told me he got it from someone else (whose name I did not know and have since forgotten) but that I should not credit that person because it wasn't his creation either. Regrettably, I do not know whom I should thank for trafoline. Searching online for trafoline did not help. There is a nearly identical version of this handout that instead uses the word "traxoline," but searching for traxoline online was inconclusive as well. I prefer the trafoline version of the handout though because I believe that traxoline is actually montilled in New Jersey.

curiously. Some smiled knowingly. Others revert to autopilot and start to answer the questions, but soon enough feel silly for having done so.

Little direction is needed from me, other than a well timed "Why did I do this?" Class dialogue is rich and productive. Feynman's ideas were detailed, although ironically, not in his words.

For the rest of the course, anytime that anyone (including me) tries to use the name of something as a substitute for an understanding of that something, we call it a bunch of trafoline. Rigor of understanding and justification of reasoning are the expectation and the norm.

WITH APOLOGIES TO DR. SEUSS

Another curriculum that I have used with teachers from the University of Washington *Physics by Inquiry* materials covers the Properties of Matter.[3] Students operationally define mass, area, volume, etc. They develop a foundation for understanding these ideas and related concepts of sinking, floating, and density. They also study balancing. For balancing, they use homemade balances and pans with square nuts as a unit of measure.

One summer I was working with a class of elementary school teachers on Properties of Matter. Many of these teachers went through a predictable sequence. They came to my class uncomfortable with science having steered away from it in the classes that they taught. They came to class unsure.

Any difficulties that they had though, including those that they had with what they thought were simple topics, were unpacked fully. Frustration built as answers were not given to them. Participants were directed to build an understanding of the process and content of the science for themselves. They struggled, but then they got it. They also got that they got it, and they appreciated it. These were dedicated teachers and learners and for many it was an emotional and meaningful experience.

Arlene was a veteran elementary school teacher who enrolled in class just because she wanted to do a better job teaching her students science. She struggled. She worked hard each day. She acted like learning science was the most important thing in the world for her, staying after class asking questions trying to understand each topic. She also stated outright that this was her first opportunity to really learn science.

While many teachers expressed their gratitude for the experience, Arlene did so in a way that particularly put a smile on my face. Arlene succeeded as much as any teacher in the class trying to figure out the balancing of square nuts. At the end of the last class, she presented me with a personally modified book. She took a copy of *Green Eggs and Ham* by Dr. Seuss. With the help of a printer, scissors, and some tape, she reconstructed the entire book as *Square Nuts in Pans*. It reflected her own journey from "I do not like that Rich I am" to "I do not like them so

---

[3] McDermott, L.C. and the Physics Education Group at the University of Washington, *Physics by Inquiry*, John Wiley & Sons, Inc., New York (1996).

confused I am, I do not like square nuts in pans" all the way through to "Thank you! Thank you, So smart I am!" I was so happy about how the teacher was appreciative of all that she learned.

ARNOLD ARONS AND REFLECTIONS ON TEACHER EDUCATION

I met Arnold Arons at the University of Washington in 1992. Both from his writings and directly from him, I was overwhelmed by his integrated knowledge of science (and everything else). He knew the scientific ideas and the thought processes detailing how those ideas came to be developed. He knew how students do and do not come to understand the content and processes of science. He also had no problem saying it the way it is.

Much of my perspective as a teacher is informed by Arons' assessment quoted at the beginning of the chapter. In politics, economics, medicine, religion, and every other walk of life ideas are delivered with booming authority regardless of merit. We all live with the consequences of a growing population unable to tell the difference. Arnold Arons saw the legitimate teaching of science by inquiry as an opportunity to develop the thinking and reasoning skills needed to move in the other direction. Calls for standards, assessments, and high achievement are desperately needed. What is needed even more is that these calls direct us towards and not away from what Arons, Feynman, Dewey, Galileo, Plato, Einstein, King, da Vinci, and even Berra have all pointed us towards.

STRATEGIES THAT WORK: TEACHER EDUCATION

Many of the strategies that I use when working with teachers are described throughout all of the earlier chapters. An additional assignment that I integrate is a follow up on an Arnold Arons reading assignment related to teaching and learning science. Excerpts from the cited article are given at the end of this chapter.

Teachers write vivid recollections exemplifying a range of science education experiences. Subsequent classroom discussion about the assignment is rich in specific details of science education, inquiry, and pedagogy.

Reflecting on critical dimensions of the teaching and learning of science `

Read the framework described by Arnold Arons for assisting the attainment of the formal operational level of intellectual development. [See below.] For each objective, describe a relevant example from your own experience as either an instructor or student. For each example that you feel models exemplary practice, explain why. For each example that you feel is a poor model, explain why and describe how you feel it should be done.

Below are excerpts of objectives from Arnold Arons article "Cultivating the capacity for formal reasoning: Objectives and procedures in an introductory physical science course"[4] relevant to the assignment above. Teachers in the class are asked to read the entire article.

(1) *Exploratory activity and question asking prior to concept formation and model building.* Examples: exploration of the phenomenology of balancing prior to induction of the quantitative relationship; exploration of conditions necessary for lighting flashlight bulbs with 1.5-V cells prior to formation of concepts such as "circuit," "current," and "resistance." Such exploration gives the students a much needed opportunity to use English in forming questions and describing observations prior to invoking technical terminology. It also provides opportunity for discrimination between observation and inference. It is necessary to watch the initial struggles towards clear expression and articulation to appreciate how little opportunity most students have had to form statements arising out of their own consciousness and experience and how much they have relied on the repetition of words drawn from others.

(2) *Idea first and name afterwards.* Examples: Counting the unit squares in an irregular surface prior to introducing the name "area" (most students consider "length x width" to be the *definition* of "area" and have no idea what to do if the surface has an irregular shape); developing evidence and examining phenomena from which one infers discreteness in the microscopic structure of matter before introducing the term "atoms"; examining thermal phenomena that lead to introduction of the concept of "heat" in addition to the concept of "temperature." Students have virtually no sense of the fact that words acquire meaning and communication becomes possible only through elements of shared experience. They almost invariably hold the unprobed assumption that knowledge and understanding reside directly in the technical terms. Competent articulation of operational definitions intelligible to another individual emerges only after repeated practice with each successive concept.

(3) *Translating words into symbols and symbols into words.* Examples: converting verbal problem statement into the corresponding arithmetical formulations; sketching position-time graphs of motions that have been described in words; interpreting the significance of linearity of graphs (such as mass vs. volume of a particular substance, circumference vs. diameter of circles, net force vs. acceleration imparted to a particular body) and recognizing the slopes as density, pi, and mass in the respective instances.

(4) *"How do we know...? Why do we believe...? What is the evidence for...?"* Examples: How do we know the earth is round? Why do we believe there are only two varieties of electrical charge? What is the evidence for discreteness rather than continuity in the structure of matter? The great

---

[4] Reprinted with permission from Arons, A.B. "Cultivating the capacity for formal reasoning: Objectives and procedures in an introductory physical science course" *Am. J. Phys.*, **44**, 834-838 (1976), Copyright 1976, American Association of Physics Teachers.

majority of students have accepted these propositions on faith. They have almost never examined the evidence or articulated in their own words any of the reasons that lead us to these views. They received them as end results from authority. Eventually it does become necessary to take some end results of scientific inquiry on faith. The students, however, have never discriminated between assertions such as "scientists know that..." and instances in which they have followed at least some of the evidence and understood how the particular result was validated and accepted. It is essential to lead them to an understanding of the basis for some of our most fundamental ideas concerning the physical world – ideas they have never realized they accepted without evidence and without understanding.

(5) *Inferences drawn from models.* Examples: How do we visualize, in terms of the kinetic molecular model, the dissolving of a substance in water? Is it possible to discriminate between the geo- and heliocentric models of the solar system on the basis of naked eye observations? Many students have great difficulty understanding that it is impossible to discriminate between two models that equally well account for the available observations. They expect to be able to "prove" the one they "know" to be correct. It is essential that students have the time to express the requisite lines of reasoning in their own words, drawing as much as possible on their own observations and experiences. Telling them the correct answers in lucid lectures, explanations, or text presentations is futile. This is what has been done before, and it has left no trace on the students' intellects.

(6) *"Backwards science: forwards science."* Examples: (a) Student: If the moon and the sun are on opposite sides of the earth when we see a full moon, *why* is the moon not eclipsed each time by the shadow of the earth? Teacher: *Because* the moon, earth, and sun are not usually in a straight line. (b) Student: Why do two bulbs connected in series burn less brightly than one bulb alone? Teacher: *Because* of the resistance of the bulbs. Each of these instances shows scientific reasoning presented to the students in a "backwards" way. A *because* answer to the *why* question carries for the student the clear implication that there existed an *a priori* reason for the phenomena. What is necessary in such instances is prompt reversal of the initial sequence. In example (a) the much more effective teacher response is: It is an observed *fact* that the full moon is not eclipsed every month; what can we infer from this observation about the character of the moon-earth-sun alignment? In (b): It is an observed *fact* that the two bulbs in series burn less brightly; what does this suggest concerning the effect of added material on the intensity of the current we visualize in the circuit?

(7) *Interpretation of the results of multiplication and division in specific contexts.* Many students do not interpret multiplication as a form of addition. For example, they do not recognize the calculation of length x width for a rectangular surface as a short way of counting the unit squares; they dredge

up "length x width" as a memorized operation. They have never interpreted division as calculating how much of the numerator is associated with one chunk of whatever is in the denominator. Example: "Suppose we find in the grocery store a box marked 75 cents and 14 ounces, what is the meaning of the number 75/14?" Many students have trouble, but the majority of students say that this is how much we pay for one ounce. "Now suppose we calculate the number 14/75." The majority of students have almost never thought about how many ounces one gets for one cent, 14/75 is a frightening, unintelligible *fraction*. After students have been led through interpreting 14/75 as the number of ounces obtained for one cent, one can usually go back to M/V and elicit the interpretation that this represents the number of grams in one cubic cm. One can then elicit the interpretation of V/M and the generalized interpretation of the result of division.

(8) *Arithmetical reasoning involving division.* Interpreting the consequences of division as illustrated in the preceding section is only the first step in a sequence. The next fruitful step is made through questions such as "We have 800 g of material having a density of 2.3 g/cm3. What must be the volume occupied?" The first impulse of most students is to manipulate the formula $\rho=M/V$. Investigation of what they are doing reveals that this is an essentially concrete operational response. They are not thinking either arithmetically or algebraically but are literally moving the concrete objects ρ and V around in a procedure they have been previously shown and laboriously memorized. The students must be led to articulate something like the following: What does 2.3 g/cm3 mean? This is the number of grams in one cubic cm of the material. We can think of 2.3 g as a package. If we find how many such packages there are in 800, we obtain the total number of cubic cm because each package is associated with one cubic cm.

TIDBITS

Reflection

Insanity is trying the same thing over and over and expecting different results.

- Author unknown

JUNE 26: LAST DAY

June 26 was my last day at UHS.[1] I thought about how much I learned in a real, challenging science classroom. For me, this was the place where the rubber meets the road.

There is so much I would do differently if I could do my first year at UHS over again. I would redouble my efforts in reaching out to school leaders, colleagues, and students with the goal of connecting to the students in every way possible right from the beginning (and even before). However, I would not beat myself up as much about things I wish were different but had no control over.

In trying to improve student approaches to learning, I would start with an understanding of how students learn. Epistemologies need to change, but it is a process. There is no doubt that I would continue to use inquiry as a focus of my approach to teaching science. If I could do it all over again, the strategies that work discussed in every chapter would be even more of a guide to the classroom activities that I would incorporate.

While I would make these changes, I realize that no matter what preparation one has for the first year in a school like UHS, it is a year to struggle with and learn from more than any other year as a teacher. I would look at each lesson, activity, relationship, and perspective as part of a process. I would look to cultivate and improve what I do between the first and second year. No matter how well (or poorly) the first year goes, I would always remind myself that the second year

---

[1] I received the results of the New York State Physics Regents for my students in late June. Even before it happened I felt that the results would be anticlimactic. My students' participation and grades turned out to be indistinguishable from most other physics teachers in my school or similar schools. In my head, any rationalization as to why they did as poorly (or as well) as they did felt like a red herring. The quest for success on the Regents is a misguided one. I do not interpret success on the Regents as worth boasting about. I do not interpret failure as worth apologizing for. Good instruction does not point to Regents success (or failure). Bad instruction does not point to Regents failure (or success). I do not know what the Regents scores tell me, good or bad. I do know though that the nature and emphasis of the test misguides the instruction itself. (I could not resist placing this information as a footnote, complete with smaller font.)

would go better. As someone who tries so hard and cares so much, this is important to remember.

Regardless of where and when I would teach though, I would NOT compromise on bringing the best education that I know how to bring to each and every student that walked into my classroom. Standardized tests would not stop me. Other people's low expectations would not stop me. Making my life easier would not stop me. The stakes are high, the time is now, and the teacher is the key to it all.

IRONY

The end of the year was a great chance to reflect on my teaching at UHS and to make connections among the different vantages that I have had in education. Much of my reflection is reflected in the 12 chapters of this book. To take it a step further, I have reflected about this reflection. I now share some of this meta-reflection.

I love being a teacher and an educator. I love that I had the opportunity to work in a meaningful, challenging environment like UHS. I feel privileged to be lucky enough to dedicate my career to education. To me that includes not only work with students and teachers, but trying to make sense of teaching and learning.

From my different perspectives, I consistently see an educational system fraught with irony. We want our students to be inquisitive lifelong learners, but we prescribe specifically what they should do, say, and write in school. We want our students to apply what they learn in class to all situations, but we create a classroom environment de-contextualized from their lives. We emphasize math and literacy fluency, but these are skills honed when students are immersed in the arts and sciences. We test to gauge success, but the way we test hinders success. We recognize that those from the most disadvantaged backgrounds need the most support, but they are the ones for whom the negative impacts of our tests are felt most harshly. We want to recruit and retain the best teachers, but we have a system which frustrates the most creative and dedicated while rewarding the most mediocre. And if there is one thing that is clearest of all, it is that the teacher is far and away the single most important determinant of the quality of the education in any classroom.

ALARMING IS NOT THE SAME AS DEPRESSING

I have sometimes heard that observations like those I share in this book are "depressing." I disagree with this choice of word. I prefer "alarming." Depressing sounds like there is nothing that can be done. Alarming sounds like consequences are high, and we must rise up to fix that which is broken. Strategies that promote genuine learning do exist and can be the focus.

At every school in which I have taught, including UHS, I have been overwhelmed by numerous teachers and students who have shown me that schools can be institutions of real learning. Mr. Diaz showed me what a great science class could look like in an inner city school. Ms. O'Brien showed me the same for a history class. Students in the Summer Scholars Program taught me that students want to be real learners and real scientists more than they want to play the game of listen-memorize-repeat. Robinson (and so many others) taught me that there is reason (and moral responsibility!) to translate the approaches of the Summer Scholars Program to all New York City classrooms. Watching Marlon play with tape made me feel that such an implementation could work in any environment, for almost any student.

I have seen so many teachers do amazing things. I have seen so many students grow in leaps and bounds. I am as excited about possibilities as I am alarmed about failures.

Great education with high standards and accountability must be accomplished in all of our schools. And it can certainly happen, even if it is not happening now.

COMMUNITY BUILDING

One way or another, I am often asked by science teachers (among others) for a prescription for improving education. When the question focuses on "What textbook should I use?" I know it will be a very short or very long conversation.

Regardless, while I am happy to engage in a discussion related to any of the chapter themes, I do not really think that there is a "prescription" for success. So instead I talk about my association with the American Association of Physics Teachers. I note how this has helped me become part of a community whose goal is to understand and improve student learning.

I encourage all teachers to participate as part of a similar professional community and become engaged in a process of inquiry themselves with the goal of learning to teach by inquiry. Then I encourage them to use an informed perspective to continuously improve their craft and impact the system.

Then I hope that those best equipped to do the most good continue to teach and speak with the loudest voice. More than any other group, current and former classroom teachers define the educational system.

QUOTES THAT I LIKED BUT DID NOT MAKE IT INTO THE BOOK
(UNLESS THIS COUNTS)

On inquiry:

They emphasize a new way of teaching and learning about science that reflects how science itself is done, emphasizing inquiry as a way of achieving knowledge and understanding about the world.

- National Science Education Standards[2]

You're not supposed to analyze it; you're supposed to blindly recite it even if it doesn't make sense, like the bible or an eye chart.

- Stephen Colbert

---

[2] National Research Council, *National Science Education Standards*, Washington, DC: National Academic Press (1996).

CHAPTER 12

On the difference between schooling and education:

I have never let my schooling interfere with my education.

   - Mark Twain

Personally I'm always ready to learn, although I do not always like being taught.

   - Winston Churchill

On the State of high school education:

The author needs to convince his readers why they should abandon methods that produce 93% of students who select the correct answer in favor of the author's method.

   - Anonymous reviewer of book draft[3]

When I think back on all the crap I learned in high school, it's a wonder I can think at all.

   - Paul Simon

On high stakes testing:

Your scores on this test will determine how much money this suck shack gets for years to come so we will spend every moment of the next 2 weeks drilling the questions and answers into your soft little skills.

   - Gary Chalmers[4]

Test scores are up.

   - Michael Bloomberg[5]

On the importance of good science teaching to our children:

Science can be introduced to children well or poorly. If poorly, children can be turned away from science; they can develop a lifelong antipathy; they will be in a far worse condition than if they had never been introduced to science at all.

   - Isaac Asimov

Preschool children almost always ask 'How do we know? Why do we believe? questions until formal education teaches them not to. Most high school and college students then have to be pushed, pulled, and cajoled into posing and examining such questions; they do not do so spontaneously.

---

[3]   Referring to relative motion of the earth and sun from chapter 2.
[4]   School Superintendent, *The Simpsons.*
[5]   New York City Mayoral Campaign re-election slogan, 2009

Rather, our usual pace of assignments and methods of testing all too frequently drive students into memorizing end results, rendering each development inert. [6,7]

　- *Arnold Arons*

On ignorance:

The only good is knowledge and the only evil is ignorance.

　- *Socrates*

Nothing in all the world is more dangerous than sincere ignorance and conscientious stupidity.

　- *Martin Luther King*

Two things are infinite: the universe and human stupidity; and I'm not sure about the universe.

　- *Albert Einstein*

On our future:

An investment in knowledge always pays the best interest.

　- *Benjamin Franklin*

The countries that out-teach us today will out-compete us tomorrow.

　- *Barak Obama*

Race To The Top is No Child Left Behind on steroids.

　- *Dianne Ravitch*

BY THE NUMBER

Number of days I was absent from UHS during school year: 1

Number of different schools in which I instructed that resulted in at least one anecdote presented: 3 high schools, 1 middle school, 1 elementary school, and 3 colleges

Number of words that I presented with dictionary definitions in this book: 2 (inquiry and epistemology)

---

[6]　Arons, A. *Teaching Introductory Physics* (John Wiley & Sons, NJ, 1997).

[7]　This might not exactly be what the youngest children are thinking when they ask repeatedly "why?" Regardless, Arons' criticism of formal education is relevant and important.

Number of equations I included (counting both versions of Coulomb's law) in this book: 8

Some of my favorite words:
Number of times that I used the word "inquiry": 81[8]
Number of times that I used the word "context": 35[9]
Number of times that I used the word "reasoning": 78
Number of times that I used the word "understanding": 116[10]

OTHER BOOK TITLES THAT I CONSIDERED

Education reform for dummies, I mean education reform for smart people

Education reform for people who suffer from a lack of education reform

Education reform for people who don't suffer from a lack of education reform

No child left behind: Hold them all back

Every child left behind: Why we need to fix schooling in America

High stakes testing, inquiry, and the need for real science education

The educational system has no clothes

Diary of a madman

Not trafoline

---

[8] Counting all uses of the word inquiry in this chapter, including the 2 times inquiry appears in this footnote.

[9] Counting other versions of the word like de-contextualized.

[10] Including authentic understanding, basic understanding, conceptual understanding, deep understanding, functional understanding, fundamental understanding, full understanding, independent understanding, meaningful understanding, operational understanding, real understanding, rigor of understanding, and scientific understanding.

CPSIA information can be obtained at www.ICGtesting.com
Printed in the USA
LVOW030926091211

258607LV00002B/3/P